An Overview of
E-E (Entertainment-Education)
and its Application
in the Cambodian Context

សេចក្ដីសង្ខេបនៃ

ការការកំសាន្ដ

និងការអនុវត្ដរបស់វា

នៅក្នុងបរិបទនៃប្រទេសកម្ពុជា

ABSTRACT

In this report, I will present an overview of an area of development communications known as Entertainment-Education (E-E), also referred to as "Edutainment". I will present a summary of E-E/Edutainment media and approaches, and a brief exploration of the various theoretical and methodological factors behind its effectiveness as an instrument for prosocial change in the development process and beyond.

I will also attempt to place E-E/Edutainment interventions in the context of general contemporary development communications strategies, while observing some strengths, as well as some shortcomings and limitations, of E-E/Edutainment as a prosocial communications approach.

Along these lines, I will occasionally incorporate relevant first-person observations made while working as a freelance media producer, consultant, and experimenter in the Cambodian LDC environment between 2005 and the present. In particular, I will offer some practical and experiential insights that are related to E-E/Edutainment production processes, which in turn may suitably compliment much of the theoretical literature gathered for this effort.

Lastly, I will offer a projection of some potential future E-E/Edutainment trends and frameworks that are likely to occur to some degree as the field develops. I will also offer a hypothesis of some ideal E-E/Edutainment interventions and media relevant to the Cambodian economic and cultural context. Ultimately, this report is intended to provide a practical introduction and point of departure for my Cambodian colleagues (and other local colleagues working in other comparable LDC scenarios) to identify, understand, and to implement the concepts introduced here. My hope would be that future E-E/Edutainment media interventions in Cambodia and other LDC environments may be devised with a more significant local design and capacity than is observable today.

ACKNOWLEDGEMENTS

I would like to thank Dorothy Kidd of the University of San Francisco for her kind assistance in introducing me to appropriate literature in the E-E (Entertainment-Education)/ Edutainment field, as I first began to explore the subject matter at hand.

I would also like to thank Professor John Pilgrim of Royal University of Phnom Penh for his feedback and responsiveness as the themes of this report developed, especially in terms of scholarly approaches to the material.

Finally, I would like to thank E-E/Edutainment scholar Dr. Arvind Singhal for his informative and thought provoking replies to my email inquiries regarding theoretical and practical aspects of the E-E/Edutainment field.

"As the twig is bent the tree inclines"

-Virgil

.   INTRODUCTION

Development Communications is a general term meant to describe the use of media as part of a development communications strategy; the World Bank defines development communications (also known as "DevComm" or even "ComDev"), as: "the integration of strategic communication in development projects." (World Bank, 2009) Development Communications can also be defined as "organized efforts to use communications processes and media to bring social and economic improvements, generally in developing countries." (Museum of Broadcast Communications, 2009)

The World Bank further notes the importance of changing behaviors and attitudes in the development process, stating that "all development requires some kind of behavior change on the part of stakeholders" (World Bank, 2009) while acknowledging the role of effective communications programs in the viability of development projects:

> Well-conceived, professionally implemented communication programs
> that are tied directly to reform efforts or development project objectives
> that bring understanding of local political, social and cultural realities to
> bear in the design of development programs can make the difference
> between a project's success and failure. (World Bank, 2009)

While early communications theorists based their strategies upon the apparent success of World War II propaganda undertakings (Museum of Broadcast Communications, 2009), the design of development communications efforts currently involve ethical components that strive to differentiate such media from propaganda, focusing instead on "authentic" prosocial message delivery for social change.

Strategic development communications aim for prosocial behavior change amongst stakeholders as a primary goal. This behavior-change component stands alongside, and distinct from, the more didactic functions of development communications, such as the dissemination of raw information. While the latter are inherently part of any development communications efforts, they alone are not sufficient for motivating the change of long established practices or behaviors amongst stakeholder communities. (Stearns and Stearns, 1988)

Development communications therefore, encompasses a vast range of media and applications utilized in development programs. This includes such varied media as: written reports, newsletters, published surveys, press releases, bumper stickers, banners, billboards, inter and intra-departmental emails, posters, radio spots, televised PSAs, brochures, action plans, webcasts, and more. In short, whatever media might be strategically utilized in development projects can be grouped under the general umbrella term, "Development Communications" or "Communications for Development" (Communications Initiative Website, 2006)

Entertainment-Education (also known by the acronym-fond development community and others as "E-E"), and often referred to colloquially as "Edutainment", is a specific, stakeholder-oriented area of development communications which is intended to bring about prosocial behavioral change in a target demographic or audience. E-E/Edutainment is, for this reason, often as a key component in strategic development programs. E-E/Edutainment may be further defined as "the intentional placement of educational content in entertainment messages (Rogers and Singhal, 2002), or as "a communication strategy consisting of the insertion of educational or motivational information into entertainment media." (Regis, St. Catherine, and Vaughan, 2000).

The Johns Hopkins Bloomberg School of Public Health, a leader in utilizing E-E/Edutainment interventions to promote health education, describes E-E/Edutainment as media which "uses drama, music, or other communication formats that engage the emotions to inform audiences and change attitudes, behavior, and social norms." (Johns Hopkins Bloomberg School of Public Health, 2008), while E-E/Edutainment scholar Dr. Arvind Singhal (2002) describes an E-E/Edutainment intervention as "the process of

purposely designing and implementing a media message to both entertain and educate, in order to increase audience members' knowledge about an educational issue, create favorable attitudes, shift social norms, and change overt behavior."

II.   RESEARCH OBJECTIVES

The objectives of this research are to identify and analyze the relevance and application of systems and methodologies of E-E/Edutainment in the Cambodian context(s), as well as other comparable LDC environments.

III.   MAIN RESEARCH QUESTIONS

1. What is E-E/Edutainment, and what part does it play in development communications?
2. What are the purposes and operational programs of social and developmental agencies in Cambodia to which specific E-E/Edutainment approaches might be applied?
3. What are the constraints on the effective design and introduction of an E-E/Edutainment strategy in Cambodia?

4. What research questions and methodology might be further developed on Cambodian education and its potential in development and social programs by Khmer researchers?

IV. LIMITATIONS OF THE STUDY

The formal, scholarly areas of Entertainment-Education (or E-E, also known as "Edutainment") were entirely new to me as I began to research this topic. However, I had fortuitously – though unwittingly - practiced many of the E-E /Edutainment approaches and concepts presented here during my experiences as a media producer throughout the course of my career.

Many of my observations working in the field in Cambodia as a media producer/experimenter and consultant are necessarily subjective, though they are verifiable. I have included them in this report to provide a balanced, pragmatic view of the realities of working in E-E/Edutainment production processes and development communications areas in this particular developing country context, where imperfect, non-classical market dynamics intersect with a very high density of donor subsidized media projects.

One significant limitation of this study was this author's lack of Khmer language *fluency*; while I maintain a strong and workable intermediate level (spoken) language proficiency, a lack of absolute native speaker-level proficiency restricted appreciation of a range of colloquial Cambodian media including Edutainment, "Quasi-Edutainment*", and "Pure" Entertainment content.

(*"Quasi-Edutainment" is coined here for the lack of a more suitable term; it is used to describe media content in the Cambodian context which "hijacks" the prosocial Edutainment genre for an ulterior aim. The prevalence of such media was pointed out to this author by a Cambodian colleague during a review of an earlier draft of this report.)

Examples of "quasi-Edutainment" include Cambodian talk shows or infommercials featuring local celebrities or hosts who demonstrate, as "experts" (but without any medical expertise), a variety of quack medicines in an apparently prosocial setting or format. Barring any viable Cambodian state mechanism to vet or quality control medical panaceas which are nonetheless promoted as bona-fide, these items are offered to the public via mass media channels as medically beneficial, when no such qualification can reasonably be made.

Further research into these areas may best be conducted by native speaking Cambodians who may more adroitly navigate localized and colloquial expressions and settings that could otherwise be lost on a foreign social scientist. This suggestion might reasonably be extended to other LDC environments as well.

The logistical limitations in producing this report were also significant. Scholarly materials on the subject of E-E/Edutainment were not available in any library or collection this researcher had been able to locate in Cambodia, and I was unable to afford to purchase and ship the necessary hardcopy books from abroad. I therefore had to rely extensively - nearly exclusively in fact - on the Internet as a means to search for and access materials.

However, Cambodia is a developing country with a poor Internet infrastructure overall.

The Internet in Cambodia is 1) relatively expensive due to high local tariffs, 2) not robust or reliable, due to connection problems and power outages, and 3) often carries download limits, with the user paying by the Megabyte beyond a pre-set limit (unless an expensive "unlimited" plan is purchase). Indeed, even the library of Royal University of Phnom Penh, where I undertook some of the research for this report, does not allow *any* downloads of materials due to financial limitations.

Therefore my strategy in gathering relevant literature had been to identify and secure relevant PDF files on the topic, so that I could then save the links and then download them at once at a local Internet café or via my laptop at other WiFi equipped venues in Phnom Penh. I could then study the literature offline at my own convenience, without buying any extra time at an Internet café - or any extra coffees at a WiFi equipped establishment in the capital.

Much of the literature cited here, therefore, is limited to whatever I could access in PDF or other portable document format, with some exceptions when I could locate a relevant dedicated websites on E-E/Edutainment or development communications. In some instances, because my online time was often "on the meter" (at about 2000 Riel, or about 50 US cents per hour), I occasionally downloaded entire websites using dedicated

website backup applications so that I could study the sites in their entirety offline, without time constraints or inconvenience posed by Internet cafes or WiFi-enabled bars or restaurants.

In instances where I sought to download E-E/Edutainment computer applications (i.e., educational games), I utilized FTP applications that allowed resumable downloads, so as to be able to retrieve these files over the course of many sessions.

Some files, such as the World Food Program's *Food Force* cited in this report, were in excess of 200 Megabytes, which is significantly large for current Cambodian Internet usage. I gradually downloaded these larger files over the course of several repeated trips, (and many cups of coffee), at a variety of WiFi enabled coffee shops in Phnom Penh.

Aside from whatever insights or conclusions can be drawn from this report, I would encourage the Cambodian Ministry of Information and Communications to improve Internet access and pricing in Cambodia by lowering the existing high tariffs rates for service providers, which are among the highest in the region.

I would also recommend that the governments of all less developed countries focus on building an improved IT infrastructure as a top priority, including better access to the Internet in rural areas and public educational institutions. Having experienced a significant digital divide firsthand in producing this report, I'm confident that such an action would yield a maximum payoff for the Cambodian nation and economy as a whole, with cost-value benefits on par with other essential infrastructure projects already regarded as being top priority tasks.

V.   LITERATURE REVIEW

E-E/Edutainment media aims to promote an agenda through the modification of individual and/or collective behavior, by way of a media vehicle which is entertaining enough to engage stakeholders while delivering specific, intentional (and presumably prosocial) messages.

E-E/Edutainment media may assume the form of: mass media, such as radio or television serials, folk media, long-form or one-off (non-serial) videos and films, New Media delivered via the Internet and mobile telephones, theater and live performances, folk and traditional media such as educational dance performances and puppet shows, and other formats.

However disparate these media forms may be, the core of any E-E/Edutainment intervention is designed to be essentially, if not primarily *entertaining*.

> Using entertainment programmes to promote pro-social messages maximizes audience exposure, liking and recall of messages in ways that might not be achievable through the use of straight-forward didactic messages. (Singhal and Svenkerud, 1994)

Prosocial telenovela pioneer Miguel Sabido asserts that televised E-E serial interventions should be primarily entertaining in order to be effective:

> The entertainment element should account for about 70 percent of the story. The methodology I created (which has become known as the "Sabido methodology") uses two of three sub-plots in a long-running serial drama to create entertainment - through changes of fortune, use of a range of human emotions, cliffhangers, compellingly well-written drama, strong acting, realistic productions, and the appropriate "tone" of the drama. (Barker and Sabido, 2005)

In order to be effective, E-E/Edutainment must be designed to actively engage the audience, user, or community member(s) in the process of delivery of core prosocial messages. As a corollary, non-entertaining, purely didactic interventions or communications programs are usually not be capable of retaining voluntary audience or stakeholder interest, no matter how well produced.

E-E/Edutainment interventions vary widely in scale and demographic of target audience. Some national mass media campaigns can reach tens or hundreds of thousands (and even millions) of viewers or radio listeners. On the other hand, non-mass media forms, such as folk or traditional media – which includes "traditional theatre or drama, masks and puppet performances, tales, proverbs, riddles and songs" - may focus on the village or neighborhood level and may seek smaller, niche audience participation. Such media are often specifically geared towards a rural and traditional audience. (Daudu, S. 2009)

Folk media used as an E-E/Edutainment vehicle may be considered "a communication vehicle for promoting and improving dialogue which the common people or rural farmers employ to deliver their messages." (Zwaal 2000, in Daudu, S. 2009)

Examples of E-E/Edutainment as components of prosocial communications strategies might include: televised serials or soap operas (also known in Latin America as a *telenovela*) which features characters facing key challenges of a primary social issue, such as AIDS/HIV; radio dramas that dramatizes gender bias issues; children's cartoons that emphasizes the importance of staying in school; puppet shows or dance troupes that brings health awareness messages to a rural community; or downloadable computer games which educate a user-player in understanding ways to manage natural resources, to name a few.

E-E/Edutainment is not designed to be didactic, and is therefore not an ideal vehicle for the delivery of raw information. The strength of E-E lies in the medium's ability to connect with the viewer, participant, or user on an emotional and experiential level (Johns Hopkins Bloomberg School of Public Health, 2008)

Barker and Sabido (2005) state that successful E-E/Edutainment interventions must be crafted so that they are entertaining enough to attract and retain viewers or users on their own volition, while still effectively delivering prosocial messages. Therefore, the media itself must focus on engaging stakeholders with media content which is primarily entertaining and non-didactic. Didactic support materials, such as media campaign posters, informational brochures, reports, supplementary teacher training guides, and other "less entertaining" content may accompany E-E media as part of an overall development communications campaign approach.

These data-heavy materials, whether intended for development practitioners or the public, are best utilized as a complimentary component of a total communications strategy or intervention.

E-E/Edutainment media is especially effective at producing prosocial behavior change when the media content—whether this be a TV or radio serial, New Media, or social issue street theater – allows a viewer, participant, or user to *identify* with a primary character in a story or narrative. Characters in a prosocial narrative are typically depicted facing a social issue or scenario which forms the basis of an educational theme or social message. The viewer or audience member identifies with a sympathetic character and thereby vicariously experiences (and learns from) the same behavior-changing scenarios that the character is facing.

Social Theorist Arturo Bandura (1969) discusses this process of identification in great detail, and this particular learning mechanism is a pivotal reason for the effectiveness of E-E/Edutainment media. Identification in this context can be described briefly as "a process in which a person patterns his thoughts, feelings, or actions after another person who serves as a model."

He further asserts that identification must be used as a key learning mechanism case during the socialization process, because relying exclusively on a trial-and-error system would often lead to "costly or fatal consequences", while stating that "If social learning proceeded exclusively on the basis of rewarding and punishing consequences, most people would never survive the socialization process." (Bandura, 1969) Prosocial behaviors, therefore, must be acquired in part during an individual's socialization process, through this process of *identification*, which entails the observation of the successful behaviors of others in society.

The Johns Hopkins Bloomberg School of Public Health (2008) cites examples of identification processes at work within its core area of health education:

> Observing others is one way that people learn and adopt a new behavior For example, a TV drama in Bangladesh, *Shabuj Chhaya*, showed couples discussing family planning and visiting a clinic for antenatal care. A radio drama in Nepal for health care providers, *Service Brings Reward*, provided information about family planning and demonstrated good counseling skills. (Johns Hopkins Bloomberg School of Public Health, 2008)

Thomas Tufte (2003) explains how identification with media personas can positively influence audience members:

In the everyday use of telenovelas, ontological security is produced through a series of mechanisms relating to the recognition of plots, persons, issues and their relevance to the public's own concerns in everyday life. Normative debates are conducted firstly in the narratives and secondly in the discussions among the public, a process by which social norms are affirmed, adapted and revised. (Tufte, 2003)

Ultimately E-E/Edutainment media aims to provoke a "shift in norms" (Singhal, 2002), leading to prosocial behavior change; Singhal (2002) asserts that such a shift in norms can be achieved in two ways:

Firstly, E-E/Edutainment "can influence audience awareness, attitudes, and behaviors toward a socially desirable end." That is, prosocially, beneficial behavior is adopted by target stakeholders following exposure to the E-E/Edutainment media - a televised public service announcement may cause viewers to give up smoking, for example.

Secondly, E-E/Edutainment "can influence the audiences' external environment to help create the necessary conditions for social change at the group or system level." An E-E/Edutainment media campaign can advocate a change or influence public policy initiatives in a prosocial direction. Singhal (2002) cites, as an example of social change on the group level, an instance where an entire village in India rejected traditional dowry practices following the broadcast of the prosocial radio soap opera, *Tinka Tinka Sukh.* (Papa, 2001, in Singhal, 2002)

Mass media forms of E-E/Edutainment, and in particular, televised prosocial soap operas and radio dramas, are particularly capable in their ability to engage an audience, by allowing viewers to identify with certain characters and themes over time, via the serial format. The serial format especially, in which a narrative is delivered in successive installments which are broadcast on a regular, periodic basis, maintains a prolonged influence amongst audience members. (Johns Hopkins School of Public Health, 2008)

Consequently, the ongoing daily lives of the fictional characters can intersect with the lives of avid viewers in ways that allow for the maximum prosocial exploitation of identification processes discussed by Bandura (1969) and others. Tufte (2003) elaborates on this phenomenon during his research on viewership of telenovelas amongst low-income women in Brazil:

> Despite often portraying a material world far from the viewers' own lives, the telenovelas touch some everyday experiences which are highly recognizable for them, thereby setting in motion identification and feelings of satisfaction and pleasure, promoting a sense of social and cultural membership of a variety of different communities, counterbalancing the many processes of socio-cultural and political-economic marginalization experienced by many low-income citizens of Brazil. (Tufte, 2003)

Arvind Singhal and Peer J. Svenkerud (1994) identify a cluster of key reasons why entertainment media is an ideal vehicle for carrying prosocial messages. Together they assert that entertainment media programs are:

> (1) *Popular,* because everybody likes to be entertained; (2) *Pervasive,* because they have a wide and growing reach; (3) *Personal,* because they can present pro-social messages in a manner that is more personal (by depicting the joys and sorrows of media characters) than might be possible in real-life; (4) *Persuasive,* because they can encourage viewers to change their attitudes and behaviours regarding a pro-social issue; (5) *Passionate,* because they can stir strong audience emotions about a pro-social issue, (6) *Profitable,* because they can attract the support of commercial advertisers; and (7) *Practical,* because they are feasible to produce. (Piotrow, 1990 in Singhal and Svenkerud, 1994; Singhal and Svenkerud, 1994)

From this author's observations working as a media practitioner in a developing country (Cambodia) from 2005 through the present, I am obliged to add qualifications to items #6, *if* we are to apply this list to E-E/Edutainment media (versus media which is "purely" entertaining).

This author has not witnessed any significant, non-subsidized, yet commercially viable televised E-E/Edutainment intervention having taken place in Cambodia between January 2005 and the present. An examination of relevant literature also does not indicate that any such E-E/Edutainment intervention has ever taken place here. Even radio E-E/Edutainment productions, which are less costly to produce than television, and therefore entail less risk in recouping production costs, are invariably largely – if not solely - supported (subsidized) by international or local non-profit groups as part of a development agenda.

In short, the relevant literature and observations in the Cambodian context have led this author to conclude that E-E/Edutainment is not a *profitable* undertaking, at least in the Cambodian LDC context – except, possibly, for the foreign producers who are hired to oversee their production by the various stakeholder development groups.

A brief survey of Cambodian-based interventions supports this conclusion:

Intervention	Type of Media	Financing Group
"Taste of Life"	TV Serial (soap)	DFID, USAID, BBC World Trust ("Taste of Life Website http://www.tasteoflifecambodia.com/)
"Punishment of Love"	TV Serial (based on previous radio serial)	DFID, USAID, PSI (The http://www.comminit.com/en/node/123705 Communications Initiative Website
"Sabai Sesame"	Children's Edutainment Program (based on "Sesame Street"	US Embassy, Phnom Penh, in association with World Education, the Educational Television Corporation (ETC), and WGBH
"The Future is in Your Hands"	Radio serial with supporting videos and PSAs	U.S. Agency for International Development, the East West Management Institute - Project on Rights and Justice, World Education through the "Options" program, the Asia Foundation, and GTZ. (Equal Access Website http://www.equalaccess.org/country-project-kh02.php)
"Especially for you, Young People"	Live one-hour radio show with embedded mini-soap	The Big Lottery Fund, UK http://www.biglotteryfund.org.uk Health Unlimited http://www.healthunlimited.org/home.html United Nations Population Fund (UNFPA)

Selected List of E-E interventions in Cambodia with Supporting Agencies

In any regard, two additional qualities might reasonably be added to the list of qualities proposed by Singhal and Svenkerud (1994), above.

Firstly, I would assert that entertainment media is *Persistent*, in that recorded media content can achieve additional broadcasts and and/or distribution well beyond its initial release, by way of diligent archiving. Recorded media may be taped, filmed, stored on hard drives (or even, in the case of folk media, memorized by an orator and handed down to subsequent generations) to be recalled and redistributed long after the original production has ended.

In the area of recorded visual media, archival quality video mastering stock, when maintained under proper conditions, can last up to fifty years before degrading. (Wheeler, 2002) While a VCD or DVD optical disc may begin to degrade within two years, it can easily be archived on more durable media to be replicated later, or re-copied at appropriate intervals without loss; so long as the archival media is sustained, the original may be indefinitely reproduced. In all instances, restoration or archive of the original media - especially digital media - on a periodic basis can indefinitely prolong the shelf life of the recorded content.

Television programs in particular may enjoy an "eternal life" in the form of re-runs, provided the original content is significantly entertaining or compelling enough to warrant its preservation. Since televised E-E/Edutainment interventions often form the armature of many strategic prosocial development initiatives, this is a point worth further examination.

Although not scholarly material in a traditional sense, the culturally progressive science fiction television series, *Star Trek* – depicting television's first inter-racial kiss, for instance -- is an interesting example of the potential persistence of media in television programming.

While launched in 1966, the original series only ran for three seasons (78 episodes) before being cancelled due to low ratings, despite an apparently robust viewer base. To the rue of the show's producers and broadcasters, the viability of this demographic was only discovered following the introduction of a revised ratings system after the program had already been cancelled. (Wikipedia, 2009)

Even so, *Star Trek* stands an excellent example of persistence in media, in that the show's greatest exposure occurred well after the initial intended production and exhibition of the program.

Realizing the apparent actual appeal (entertainment value) of the original series, the owners of the program commenced re-broadcasts in 1972. These re-broadcasts, or "re-runs", have continued uninterrupted to the present. Therefore, the program's re-broadcast exposure has persisted continuously for **thirty seven years**, reaching millions of viewers in over 150 domestic and 60 international markets. Moreover, the media content has been repurposed into a wide variety of forms, including sequels, cartoons, and other content. (Wikipedia, 2009)

The *persistence* of the media content in this popular culture example is notable* in that the bulk of exposure of content occurred long after initial broadcasts ceased – and presumably, long beyond the initial expectations of the show's producers.

(*Far eclipsing the persistence of *Star Trek*, of course, are the numerous stories, fables, and epic poems existing within the oral folk media traditions around the world; many of these spoken word or sung media items have endured for hundreds, if not thousands, of years.)

This author would also assert, as a corollary to a quality of *Persistence*, that E-E/Edutainment media may also be considered *Portable* in its recorded or replicated variations. Recorded (versus live) radio dramas and televised interventions, motion pictures, comic books, and other replicable formats may be easily be shared and swapped, either in their original formats or through an intermediary, more replicable (i.e., digital) media.

For example, a telenovela, originally broadcast as a mass media series, may be re-distributed as a VCD or DVD, bypassing any need to be re-broadcast the content in order for that media to exert an influence on a viewer. Similarly, a hardcopy E-E/Edutainment comic book or magazine can be scanned and re-distributed as a PDF file or on a CD-Rom. The text may be also recorded and distributed as an audio file, or blogged and replicated ad infinitum.

Archived E-E/Edutainment media content can be repurposed, reformatted, and shared to suit a variety of purposes at a later date; this is particularly apparent in the age of digital media. Only live E-E/Edutainment interventions retain the aura of singularity that Walter Benjamin (2002) so aptly refers to in his 1936 work, *The Work of Art in the Age of Mechanical Reproduction*:

> According to Benjamin, this aura inheres not in the object itself but rather in external attributes such as its known line of ownership, its restricted exhibition, its publicized authenticity, or its cultural value. (Wikipedia, 2009)

However, even live performance E-E/Edutainment interventions such as street and community theater and puppet shows, can be recorded and exhibited again at a later date, or delivered remotely to a community on a recordable video format such as VHS, VCD, or DVD.

E-E/Edutainment differs from "pure" entertainment media, in that the social issue messages contained within the content are central to the purpose and intention behind the production.

Media which is solely entertaining exists without an overt or intentional educational agenda, and as such is not constrained to deliver any particular social message. The overarching goal of entertainment media is to retain an audience in the case of mass media in order to attract advertisers or subscribers, in the case of cable TV, or to sell units of a program or other content (for example, a computer game).

This commercial imperative often leads to the production of media content which does not contain significant prosocial content, and which may be dominated by gratuitous violence, sex, or other antisocial messages in order to attract and retain consumers. (Cyber College, 2007)

In 1992, TV Guide commissioned a study of a typical 18-hour TV broadcast day to determine levels of violence. The networks and the more popular cable channels were monitored for "purposeful, overt, deliberate behavior involving physical force or weapons against other individuals."

However, even pure entertainment vehicles which do not set out to deliver prosocial messages as part of a communications strategy, sometimes do verge onto the terrain of E-E when engaged in **social marketing** - that is, when it is commercially expedient to discuss an issue that has some current prosocial relevance.

Social marketing takes place when a key social issue or trend (for example, global warming) is exploited for its sympathetic recognition value amongst a target audience, users, or consumers. According to researcher Puja Mahesh (2007) "social marketing is the application of commercial marketing concepts and techniques to target populations to achieve the goal of positive social change."

Thomas Tufte (2003) clarifies these genealogical linkages between Edutainment and social marketing:

> Social marketing is one of the key origins of today's E-E strategies. The use of social marketing developed in the 1970s and was quickly tied up with fictional genres, and entertainment was particularly linked to mass media-based strategies, not least television and radio.

In entertainment programming, however, a social issue may be discussed or dramatized so long as it remains topically relevant to a viewer or consumer – and any particular social issue discussion may be discarded at will in favor of a new one (or none at all).

Unlike E-E/Edutainment media, which delivers prosocial messages according to a strategy designed to effect measurable prosocial behavioral change in target stakeholders, entertainment media, which may arbitrarily utilize social marketing to deliver prosocial content, is not chiefly concerned with - nor obligated to deliver - behavioral change amongst viewers, users, consumers, or stakeholders.

In short, both E-E/Edutainment and entertainment media may utilize prosocial messages and content, but entertainment media does so when it is likely to favorably impact the commercial attractiveness of the content. Similarly, entertainment media is not obliged to deliver prosocial messages by way of any mandate, and may equally discard a particular message or adopt a new one to satisfy viewers and advertisers

VI.   METHODOLOGY

The methodologies employed in this research are those of literature review and participant observation. Literature search, and especially internet search, has proved effective in examining and analyzing a large body of material from the work of researchers and practitioners operating in environments, ranging from that of change agencies and popular entertainment media in the United States, to that of prosocial development agencies employing a variety of E-E/Edutainment approaches in developing countries and beyond.

Participant observation has been used by the researcher via personal involvement as a designer and director of media and video in Cambodia, particularly in identifying problems of communication and access in the context of a rapidly evolving immersion of Cambodian professionals and agencies in IT systems and in the development of an endogenous media industry.

VI.i   WORKING HYPOTHESIS

The proposed research sets out to test the hypothesis that:

1) socially useful messages require first that they are adapted to the entertainment and general behavior patterns of the target audience; and

2) Innovative prosocial practices conveyed via E-E/Edutainment messages will be adopted at different rates by members of a social system depending on the educational level of the individual and other factors.

VI.ii   RESEARCH METHODS

To test this hypothesis, the research will be undertaken in two forms, the first of which has been carried out by the researcher in the preparation of this paper as follows:

1) a *Review* of different forms of E-Edutainment Media and their practicality in a Cambodian context;

A second component, intended for further research in the future will be:

2) a *Knowledge, Attitude and Practice* (KAP) survey among Cambodian motodop (freelance unlicensed motorcycle taxi) drivers.   The E-E/Edutainment medium used in the study will be that of messages concerning safe sex printed on the backs of playing cards – card-playing and other forms of petty gambling being a common form of entertainment for motodops while waiting for customers.

The format for this experimental E-E/Edutainment approach is explained further in Chapter VI.ii.2.

VI.ii.1. REVIEW OF DIFFERENT FORMS OF E-E/EDUTAINMENT MEDIA

Historically, many E-E/Edutainment media interventions were designed to reach as wide an audience as possible, and were therefore devised to be delivered through mass media formats such as radio and television, often in the form of serial dramas or soap operas (also called *telenovelas* in Latin American). While much of the available literature which discusses E-E/Edutainment focuses on the mass media forms - to the point that E-E/Edutainment scholarship may appear to be preoccupied with televised serial formats exclusively - the E-E/Edutainment practitioner can access a very wide range of media relevant to many uses and applications.

E-E/Edutainment may be delivered in virtually any format, depending on factors such as intended target audience, objectives of the program, and budget. (Johns Hopkins School of Public Health, 2008) These formats include, but are not limited to: mass media dramas (radio and TV); public service announcements (PSAs) or advertising spots; situation comedies; feature films; popular music; reality programming; magazine or variety programs; theater and street theater; forum theater or interactive theater; animated cartoons, comic books, and photonovelas; and Internet and mobile phone programming.

Each have distinct strengths in appealing to particular target demographics and stakeholders, and may be particularly effective when used in tandem to support an overall communications strategy.

Different media forms are commonly employed in a mutually reinforcing strategic communications strategy. For example, health-related storylines in television or radio serial E-E/Edutainment interventions may have an even greater impact when broadcast in tandem with accompanying public service announcement (PSA), and/or a telephone number where viewers can seek additional information. (Murphy, S. and Cody, M., 2003)

> Different kinds of E-E are more suitable for different contexts and budgets; mass media formats reach people who have access to radios or televisions. Young people are a prime audience for popular music. Theater, and especially street theater, reaches people without access to radio or TV. Mass media projects can be costly. In contrast, a community-level activity may cost little. Projects often use several formats or media to reach the intended audience. (Johns Hopkins Bloomberg School of Public Health, 2008)

TELEVISION

Of all the varied media formats, televised E-E interventions, especially in the form of serial programming such as soap operas or telenovelas, are generally considered to have the greatest potential for rapid behavioral change amongst stakeholder communities (Tufte, 2003). While radio can target and reach the same audience numbers (if not more, due the relative low cost of a radio versus a television set in many LDC environments), the visual/emotional engagement potential of television is unrivaled by current mass media formats.

Supporting the prevalence of TV as a chief mass media format, Brown and Singhal (1990) note the significant increase in TV sets worldwide, especially in developing countries, since the 1960s:

In Third World (ed. Developing) nations, the percentage of the world's total number of television sets increased from 5 percent in 1965, to 10 percent in 1975, to 20 percent in 1984, and to 40 percent in 1988. During the eight year period from 1980 to 1987, the number of television sets increased by 15 times in the People's Republic of China, and by 10 times in India. Television now reaches 550 million of China's 1.1 billion people (50%), about 120 million people in India (15%), and about 70 million people in Mexico (87%). (Brown and Singhal, 1990)

The capability of televised mass media to deliver prosocial messages is not only relevant to developing countries. In 2003, the Centers for Disease Control Prevention hosted a conference to gain a better understanding of the potential for TV shows to encourage positive health effects among African American and Hispanic audiences in the United States:

The mass media in general, and television in particular, provide enormous amounts of information about health through storylines in entertainment programming. (Murphy, S. and Cody, M., 2003)

By producing E-E/Edutainment in a mass media delivery format, an extremely large audience can be reached with the potential for wide-reaching and rapid change in behaviors amongst those target stakeholders. (Johns Hopkins School of Public Health, 2008)

The number of viewers exposed to a successful televised program can be staggering; the Chinese prosocial TV serial drama, *Ke Wang*, for instance, was estimated to have reached an audience of ***500 Million*** viewers. With a per-episode budget of $4650, and requiring only four days to produce each episode, the program was exceptionally cost effective on a per-viewer-reached basis, considering the number of viewers who tuned in to the program. (Singhal and Wang, 1992)

While such a scale of economy might only be realized in hugely populated countries like China or India, similarly massive audiences have been realized in Latin America, especially during the re-broadcast of particularly popular telenovelas in neighboring Latin American countries which share a common language and similar cultures. (Singhal and Wang, 1992)

The Soul City Institute for Health and Development Communication, an NGO headquartered in Johannesburg, South Africa, is notable for having produced one of the most successful multi-media E-E interventions in recent years, the *Soul City* initiative.

A carefully devised communications strategy was crucial in ensuring maximum exposure to the *Soul City* intervention's prosocial content. Over a number of seasons, the show addressed a wide range of key issues including HIV prevention, land reform, child health, tuberculoses, alcohol abuse, violence prevention, hypertension, personal finance, and small business development. (Singhal, 2002)

Primary to the successful delivery of prosocial messages were the two mass media (Radio and TV) components. A 13-part televised drama was broadcast on SABC 1, South Africa's most popular TV station, while a 60-episode radio was broadcast in numerous local languages to maximizing regional coverage.

However, the success of the coordinated *Soul City* television and radio intervention owes a great deal as well to its supporting multi-media materials. Approximately 2.5 million health education booklets based on the popularity of the TV series' characters were distributed major newspapers nationally to support broadcast media. During broadcasts, a call-in help line provided a channel for direct viewer feedback and inquiry. Additionally, following each season's broadcasts, Soul City hosted talent searches, called *Soul City Search for Stars*, to discover talent for participation in upcoming television and radio productions. (Singhal, 2002)

The series ultimately reached over 16 million people in South Africa through the coordinated radio, television and print campaigns, with a 79 percent penetration among its target audience. The show was also very popular in its own right as entertainment, achieving top audience ratings and winning six awards, including a prize for South Africa's Best Television Drama.

In order to reach a wide audience – and therefore fulfill its communication mission and justify production costs – mass media E-E/Edutainment interventions must be, as Miguel Sabido emphasizes, *significantly entertaining* in order to attract and retain viewers and listeners. (ICT for Development, 2009) This is especially true when a show may be airing at prime time and competing against the resistances of commercially driven "pure entertainment" programming.

A highly optimized E-E/Edutainment intervention, such as the successful South African *Soul City,* carries its key social issue message carefully embedded within genuinely entertaining media content. In the case of *Soul City*, an extraordinary number of viewers tuned in regularly on their own volition, bypassing other competing entertainment media programming choices which were also available.

E-E/Edutainment interventions using mass media formats such as TV and radio are typically produced in a serial, dramatic format. The television serial, soap opera (aka, "soap"), or telenovela, is an ongoing, melodramatic format which lends itself well to prosocial applications due to the number of characters who inhabit the program, which may be delivered over a considerable course of time.

34

A *telenovela* is a limited-run television serial melodrama of the type made famous in Latin America. The word is a portmanteau of tele, short for television, and novela ("novel/soap opera"). Telenovelas are essentially soap operas in miniseries format. (Wikipedia, 2009)

Soap operas are so-called, incidentally, because production costs of early programs were underwritten in their entirety by a particular company -- often a soap company or other related firm promoting products geared towards a primarily female householder demographic.

A serial drama, or soap opera, is a continuing story, usually presented on radio or TV once a week for 6 to 12 months or more. A shorter version, the miniseries, generally comprises four to six episodes. (Johns Hopkins Bloomberg School of Public Health, 2008)

The serial drama format offers significant opportunities to create identification between the viewer and fictionalized media characters, which in turn allows for effective delivery of prosocial, behavior-changing messages:

The continuing story allows for the creation of a lifelike social context and characters that change slowly and face successes and setbacks as in real life. Audiences have time to get to know the characters and identify with them. With a main plot and several subplots, the serial drama can explore issues in-depth and from the perspective of several characters. (Johns Hopkins School of Public Health, 2008)

Mass media formats are generally cost-effective, although they are typically expensive and/or complex to produce compared to other non-mass media efforts. However, a successful televised E-E/Edutainment intervention, such as *Soul City*, offers enormous reach and audience penetration, and therefore exacts a very high level of impact-per-dollar spent. Factoring in any advertising or ancillary revenue

35

recouped after production, the media costs very little to produce, on a per-person reached basis – sometimes US$3 or less to influence a viewer towards prosocial behavior change. (Johns Hopkins Bloomberg School of Public Health, 2008)

Despite the relatively high cost of production in terms of initial outlay (versus, say, street theater or other less complex Edutainment media), televised E-E/Edutainment mass media interventions continue to be produced each year worldwide, due to the impact and engagement level of the format and the potentially large audiences which can be reached.

The tradeoff for accessing the most far reaching and most powerful of mass media formats – television -- is that program content delivered by a commercial broadcast platform must conform itself, to some degree, to both the demands of the medium and to the realities of the revenue-driven broadcast model. Even a highly subsidized E-E/Edutainment program which pays for time "out of (a donor's) pocket", and which may not have to recoup production costs, still must be able to attract and retain viewers to fulfill its mission.

RADIO

Despite its impact and cost effectiveness on a per-viewer-reached basis, the high overall production costs for televised serial interventions tend to limit their production to well capitalized groups with adequate donor funding which may be conditional in one or several dimensions.   Additionally, television broadcast platforms are often subject to greater control and censorship from powerful stakeholders in both developing and developed countries alike. (Niedermier, Novotny, Alivia, Papdopoulous, Pawuk, Pope, Ralston, and Sipe, 2004)

Radio, therefore, remains another strong option for delivering prosocial content in a cost-effective mass media serial format. While not as high profile as televised content, radio interventions generally cost less to produce and can even enjoy superior audience penetration than TV, especially in rural areas where target stakeholders may be too poor to own a TV set.

> In most developing countries radio will remain the principal medium for communication in the rural areas. These are readily available, inexpensive, portable, and can have wide reach, even in very remote areas. It has high potential to be the vehicle for new agriculture ideas and technologies, especially when the content is developed with high appeal. (Chien, Escalada, Heong, Huan, Ky Ba, Quynh, and Thiet, 2008)

The NGO Minga Peru, for example, has produced the E-E/Edutainment mass media series, *Bienvenida Salud* (*Welcome Health*) since 1997. Local radio stations in the remote Peruvian Amazon broadcast the 30-minute show three times a week to a regular audience of up to 25,000 listeners. (Johns Hopkins Bloomberg School of Public Health, 2008) The Indian Edutainment radio drama, *Tinka Tinka Sukh* was a 104-episode radio serial broadcast twice weekly, from February 1996 to February 1997. The program reached seven Indian states in the population-dense Hindi-speaking area of northern India: Uttar Pradesh, Bihar, Madhya Pradesh, Rajasthan, Haryana, Himachal Pradesh and Delhi. An estimated 600 million people from 100 million households live in these states. (Brown and Singhal, 1990)

E-E/Edutainment researchers Law and Singhal (1990) conducted a sample survey in the state of Uttar Pradesh, and concluded that *Tinka Tinka Sukh* had a regular listenership of 36-40 million people in this region alone – possibly the largest listenership for any radio drama serial program worldwide.

The favorable cost structure of radio production enables less well-capitalized groups, such as Minga Peru, to undertake a radio intervention when they would not be able to afford a televised drama. Therefore, radio retains a quality which is beneficial to smaller production entities with limited budgets, or those who seek to avoid undue donor or investor influence over programming choices.

Radio is also frequently deemed to be a less "threatening" form of media in many developing governments, presumably due to its perceived role as being secondary in reach and impact to television. A Cambodian-based NGO, LICADHO explains this trend in the Cambodian context:

> Television is arguably the most popular media in Cambodia and, because of its wide appeal and the power of the moving image, the most tightly controlled of all the media forms. (LICADHO, 2008)

And furthermore –

> Every one of the country's seven TV stations is owned or closely affiliated to the government, and more particularly to the CPP (ed. - Cambodian People's Party) (LICADHO, 2008)

Radio in Cambodia does tend accommodate a greater degree of independence and freedom of expression. According to LICADHO (2008) while every TV station in Cambodia is affiliated with one political party or another, there exists a pair of truly independent radio stations: Beehive Radio, and Women's Media Center FM 102.

The Women's Media Center radio station is operated by an eponymous NGO, and often (apparently, according to the LICADHO report) avoids broadcasting significant criticism of the government on a voluntary basis. Beehive Radio, however, is not only one of the most popular stations in Cambodia, but also frequently airs perspectives that critique the government.

Mam Sonando, the owner of Beehive Radio has been imprisoned twice, and the station shut down several times – yet continues to operate and maintain a significant audience. (LICADHO, 2008)

Whether televised or broadcast by radio, mass media E-E/Edutainment serials are not confined to dramatic and melodramatic genres only. Situation comedies are also employed to deliver E-E content, although comedies are not as common as dramas - it is generally considered to be "more difficult to present serious subjects in a comedic environment" (Johns Hopkins Bloomberg School of Public Health, 2008). Usually, the comedic elements are best left to a minority of "stock" characters, while the more nuanced, essential content is delivered through more mainstream, "straight" characters.

In the Jordanian sit-com, *The 9th Circle*, for example, the comic characters are restaurant employees who do not actually deliver any essential information, providing mainly comic relief for otherwise serious health related discussions. The non-comedic customers of the restaurant explain and promote the benefits of family planning to each other, while leaving the comedic elements to the restaurant employees. Therefore, the entertaining core of the programming is held together by the fairly info-anemic, yet fun-to-watch employees of the restaurant. (Zawya, 2009)

Non-subsidized (i.e., commercial) pro-social mass media *must* remain essentially entertaining for very practical reasons: if viewers are lost, then advertisers will pull their ads and the program may be cancelled due to a loss in ad revenue.

Programming that is sponsored or financed primarily by a donor agency (subsidized) and which is not reliant upon ad-revenue to sustain production costs - as is the case in many developing countries with non-classic economies - may have more leeway while avoiding the commercial imperatives of the marketplace.

In summary, Radio, while still maintaining a potential to reach vast numbers of listeners (especially listeners in rural areas) costs less to produce than televised E-E/ Edutainment. Radio E-E/Edutainment productions are therefore more accessible to less capitalized groups who may not otherwise be able to afford to produce televised content.

VIDEO

Another key delivery format in E-E/Edutainment media is video, whether used to deliver original one-off (non-series) programming or to repurpose and redistribute serial programming that has been produced for broadcast TV.

In the development communications arena, video is often used to produce and deliver programs which are intended to raise awareness among target communities relating to key social issues. These videos are then distributed to stakeholder communities and donors alike, either as a VCD (Video Compact Disc), a DVD (Digital Versatile Disc or Digital Video Disc), or via mobile screening systems such as video vans which travel to rural areas and exhibit motion picture content on location.

While the number of video units distributed (usually via VCD or DVD) can be in the tens of thousands, and the number of viewers attending any particular mobile screening may number in the hundreds or thousands, video is not generally considered to be "mass media", as it is not electronically broadcast to a significant number of viewers over a broad geographical area. Some crossover to these definitions may occur when and if the video is later streamed online or made available as VOD (Video On Demand).

Video, especially when distributed via the VCD and DVD formats, is an excellent medium for conveying E-E/Edutainment content since it is extremely *portable*. Though video is not be considered a mass media format, it can be considered a "community media" format, especially when viewing sessions are conducted in large groups:

> In areas without access to mass media, mobile film units have brought variety shows about family planning, child survival, and HIV prevention to thousands of people. In Bangladesh, for example, such units show informational films, dramas, testimonials by local leaders, and product advertising. They also show feature films, music videos, and news and sports clips for pure entertainment. (Ngenge, T. 2003)

The mobile video concept is not confined to the non-profit or development sector either; commercial applications for mobile video abound, demonstrating the popularity of this approach:

> Meanwhile, in Mozambique, thousands of small businessmen and women have invested in a video and television set and a solar power unit or generator and are making their living by projecting films. There is an enormous possibility here. Through these small "video canteens" thousands of communities can be reached. (Ngenge, T. 2003)

The VCD format in particular lends itself towards an expanded viewing audience through repeated copying and sharing, whether the media contained is educational or strictly entertainment-oriented. Curiously, the DVD, which utilizes the MPEG-2 (Motion Picture Engineering Group - 2) format to deliver video content on an optical disc, and which has better quality than a VCD due to the less-lossy MPEG-2 compression algorithm (versus the VCD's inferior MPEG – 1 compression scheme), the DVD has a far more restricted user base in rural areas of Asia when compared to the VCD (AsiaPulse News, 2000).

An informal survey of video sellers' shops in Cambodia confirms this. This author has browsed a range of such shops, usually small wooden or thatched roadside stands with a selection of videos on disc available for purchase or for rent. A variety of Hollywood movies, Asian action films, Karaoke videos, local love stories, and other popular and "pure entertainment" content (including, less prominently, occasional pornography) populate most sellers' stores.

This author has observed little or no media relevant to development communications or E-E/Edutainment purposes on offer at any of these shops at any, with the possible (vaguely related) exception of an assortment of made-for-TV nature documentaries.

The shops all have one main thing in common, however: the medium of choice is the VCD. Only in Phnom Penh and other expatriate enclaves have I observed (pirated) DVDs being sold as the primarily video format, with titles available according to the tastes and preferences of foreign residents and tourists. The only DVD this author has ever observed for sale at a rural Cambodian video seller's stand was a Sin Sinsimouth* DVD in Kampot province in 2009. (*Mr. Sinsimouth is an iconic Cambodian singer who might be equated, in Western terms, as a star verging on national heroic status, with the stature of an Elvis Presley-plus-Frank Sinatra rolled into one)

The limited penetration of the DVD format in Cambodia, and in other developing countries where the VCD format is dominant, is likely due to several factors including:

1) the cost of the player; a DVD player costs significantly more than a VCD player

2) the cost of the blank discs, used for making copies; DVD blanks cost anywhere from two to four times as much as a blank CD-Rom

3) a relative indifference amongst viewers to the lower quality video that a VCD delivers, especially considering factors #1 and #2 (Author's interview with video shop proprietors, Kampot Province, Cambodia, November 2009)

A comparison of both formats offers clues as to why the VCD is more popular, in the Cambodian context and beyond. Though the encoded MPEG-1 video found on a VCD is lossier (has less quality) than a DVD, the resulting file size of the video is small enough to fit on a standard CD blank. The higher-fidelity, less-lossy MPEG-2 format pays for its superior quality with a much greater file size of the encoded video content, occupying up to 4.2 Gigabytes on the DVD - R or DVD-5 glass mastered format. (DVD Burning Biz, 2004)

Therefore: a feature film, encoded to be delivered via VCD format using the MPEG-1 compression standard, may fit on a single standard CD blank. The same feature film, if encoded for DVD using MPEG-2 at a high quality setting, could require up to 4.2 Gigabytes, the limits of the standard DVD blank disc, with five and a half times the capacity than a CD blank. (VideoHelp.com 1999-2007)

In summary, the video format of choice in rural Cambodia – and much of the urban areas as well, due to user base imperatives - is the VCD. Factors such as file size limitations, the comparative cost of the players, the scarcity of built-in DVD burners in second hand computers (which double as burning stations to make more copies for sale or trade), and the capacity of the ubiquitous, cheaper CD blanks versus more expensive DVD blanks have all conspired to make the VCD the current video format of choice in Cambodia (especially in rural areas), and in many other parts of Asia as well.

Interestingly, in Uganda, however, video halls are still chiefly operated using the VHS tape-based formats (Ngenge, T. 2003). VHS is also an affordable and widely available medium which can also be copied fairy easily. A VHS tape, though second-generation technology, is actually more robust in many ways to optical disc based media, since scratches on the surface of an optical disc can render it unplayable – whereas a VHS tape, if broken or cut, can actually be physically respliced with tape and can still be playable (author's experience).

However, the replication of VHS tapes on a consumer or prosumer level can usually only be done in real-time; i.e., an hour long VHS tape requires an hour to dub to a second generation, assuming a lack of high-speed professional replication equipment. This analog limitation reduces the opportunities available for secondary distribution via auto-replication*, a quality which this author hypothesizes could be exploited to enhance standard distribution of sufficiently entertaining E-E/Edutainment media.

(*Conceptually, "auto-replication" is used here synonymously with the concept of intentional "viral" media replication. However, this author proposes the term "auto-replication" due to sensitivities in terminology in light of many developing nations' AIDS/HIV awareness media education efforts.)

Whether the format is VCD, DVD, or VHS, a program that is entertaining enough, whether a nature program, strategic E-E/Edutainment media, an action film, or pornography, will often be copied and re-distributed to other users as the video content is shared, swapped, traded, sold, and otherwise circulated.

This author hypothesizes that a sufficiently entertaining E-E/Edutainment program will be re-distributed by users (or "auto-replicated") to such a degree that the content may achieve significant additional audience exposure beyond that originally envisioned or implemented by development communications strategists. Widely auto-replicated media could then reach larger audiences beyond the community level, verging on mass media levels of exposure, but without any broadcast infrastructure.

The auto-replication scenarios behind VCD use and exhibition in the Cambodian context is a core hypothesis behind the PILGRIM PROJECT, a hardware-based interface that is currently being explored by Camerado, the sponsor of this report (more information at http://www.camerado.com).

In summary, video is a robust and flexible delivery vehicle for E-E/Edutainment content. In the developing country context, low cost, easily-replicable formats such as the VCD in Cambodia and elsewhere in Asia enjoy particularly wide usage in rural areas, a quality that might be further exploited in a comprehensive distribution strategy.

POPULAR MUSIC

Popular music and music videos can effectively target a younger or teenage demographic while carrying prosocial messages tailored to their needs. Early E-E/Edutainment songs and music videos included *Cuando Estemos Juntos* ("When We Are Together") and *Detente* ("Wait") by Tatiana and Johnny, recorded and performed in Mexico in the 1980s. The songs encouraged young people to wait before having sex or becoming pregnant. Both songs were chart-toppers in Mexico and other Latin American countries. (Ngenge, T. 2003)

Karaoke in Cambodia and other Asian developing nations continues to hold promise as a niche genre for delivering E-E/Edutainment content due to its enormous local popularity. (Mok, K.D., 2009) Karaoke videos frequently portray young couples in various instances of seeking, finding, or losing each others' love; these videos therefore have an inherent capacity for directing health content messages towards issues, such as HIV/AIDS awareness, towards this demographic. The Cambodian-based NGO, RDI, is currently implementing this concept via the Karaoke video format. (RDI Cambodia, 2009)

THEATER / STREET THEATER

Theater and street (or public) theater interventions are performed live, and usually require no advanced technology to undertake.

Organized theater is one of the oldest community forms of expression, dating back to approximately 500 B.C. (Crystalinks.com, 2009) Even people without access to radio or TV can watch and vicariously participate, through character identification, while a prosocial drama unfolds before them:

> Theater can quickly and powerfully draw people's attention to an important health topic such as family planning, female genital cutting, violence against women, or HIV prevention. People without access to radio or TV can watch. (Johns Hopkins School of Public Health, 2008)

The talent of the playwright and actors (and non-actors) to successfully execute an entertaining drama which also delivers targeted social issue messages is one challenge of the form; another is the ability to quantify its impact through the automated ratings systems that other media formats enjoy. However, as we have seen regarding the popularity of the VCD video format in Cambodia and other areas of rural Asia, many nonprofessional communities do not seem to mind lapses in production values, so long as the content is compelling ("entertaining") overall.

Additionally, community members often look forward to the appearance of "their own people" on stage, versus the appearance outsiders, unless those outsiders are highly visible, famous, or recognizable stars. Interactive, or Forum Theater, is conceptually based upon Augusto Boal's "Theater of the Oppressed", (Boal, 1993) which invites the audience to participate in a production as actors – versus watching only as a non-engaged spectator - in order to break down conceptual barriers between passive spectators and the actor-change agents involved in producing a social change drama. (Johns Hopkins School of Public Health, 2008)

Thus, street/public theater remains a valid format for undertaking E-E/Edutainment interventions in local communities the world over, especially on the local and community levels.

In Bolivia, *Teatro Trono* enlists street children to perform plays for other street children to educate them about the dangers of drug use, while communicating ways to increase self-esteem, improve leadership qualities, and achieve gender equity. (Ngenge, 2003)

The Adhola United Cultural Performers (AUCP) is one of thirty-two farmer groups around Tororo, Uganda, that has been trained by the Ndere dance and theatre group to communicate prosocial messages and themes. Justine Ayo, coordinator of the troupe, attests to the power of narrative functions in communicating messages effectively, stating: "People love listening to stories, it's a traditional thing."

But aside from being entertaining, the plays educate the public about issues relevant to the local community, such as hygiene and sanitation, livestock diseases, operational aspects of farming activities - such as how to operate and maintain boreholes - domestic violence, family planning and HIV/AIDS. (Tulp and de Jager, 2009)

Live theater, which depends upon its audience for presence and impact (and which arguably *could not exist without an audience* on a phenomenological level) is a more immediate form than mass-media, and is in any case less confined to the "one-way" information flows that typify mass media propagation. (Singhal and Svenkerud, 1994)

As mentioned, Theater of the Oppressed (TO) exploits this audience-performer dynamic to its utmost limit. As part of its core aim of actualizing the ideas and inputs of an of a potentially passive, "spectator-only" audience, TO performances often invite audience members onstage to perform ad lib, thereby further breaking down any barriers between the change agent and stakeholder audience members. This quality is unique to live performance interventions. (Boal, 1993)

Offshoots of theater, street theater, and interactive theater include puppetry, songs, and other folk performances which can effectively utilize themes and crafts that are native or familiar to a local community.

BOOKS / COMIC BOOKS

Comic books, graphic novels, photonovelas, and small, low-fi (photocopied) magazines called "zines" can be utilized as E-E/Edutainment media on their own, or as support materials for a larger, strategically integrated multimedia intervention. These printed media forms can be relatively simple and inexpensive to produce, yet when printed en masse they can reach a very wide audience.

UNICEF's *Meena* series is an excellent example of a mass media intervention which incorporates comic books as supporting materials. An animated E-E/Edutainment cartoon about the adventures and challenges of a young South Asian young girl named Meena, the eponymous UNICEF-funded series promotes equal treatment of girls in education, and access to health services, while educating against too early marriage and pregnancy. (UNICEF, 2009)

The *Meena* project is also innovative in that it is designed to be self-commercializing, in an effort to be truly self-sustaining. Although launched as a donor-supported initiative, ancillary products and media are eventually to be sold as per normal commercial undertakings, with UNICEF holding the basic branding rights for commercializing the content and driving revenue. Post-broadcast assessments of *Meena* have determined that the series is effective in changing attitudes and behaviors amongst parents, leading to more equal treatment of their boys and girls, and thereby bypassing traditional gender roles. (UNICEF, 2009)

While the comic book or graphic novel format is often used only as a supplement to an overall E-E/Edutainment communications strategy, the portability of the books and their relatively low production costs make them attractive as a part of a comprehensive E-E/Edutainment intervention.

FOLK & TRADITIONAL MEDIA

Folk and traditional media, which includes "traditional theatre or drama, masks and puppet performances, tales, proverbs, riddles and songs", (Daudu, 2009) amongst other forms, can play a very strong role in E-E interventions, especially helping to validate newer media forms amongst a traditional audience. Folk media is "the media for the people, the mass of people most deprived of specific massages". (Fernandez 1996, in Daudu, 2009)

In his paper, *Folk Media and Rural Development*, Dr. Harish Kumar (2006) explains that one of the first significant international recognitions of the use of traditional (aka "folk") media in the development communications strategies occurred in 1972, when the International Planned Parenthood Federation and UNESCO organized in a series of meetings in London on the integrated use of the folk and the mass media in family planning communications. He points out the important complimentary functions of traditional/folk media in larger, mass media interventions in India:

Even when modern media have penetrated isolated areas, the older forms maintain their validity, particularly when used to influence attitudes, instigate action and promote change. (Many Voices One World, in Kumar, 2006)

As mentioned, mass media interventions such as radio or television dramas can include folk media elements embedded within the more modern media format. A traditional or indigenous character or setting featured in a mass media E-E/Edutainment intervention can make the storyline more accessible to traditional viewers, by offering them a familiar (traditional) armature for their attention.

Folk media represents the people in their natural habitat, with all their contradictions and multifarious activities. It gives a glimpse of their style of speech, music, dance, dress and wisdom. It contains of reach store of mythological heroes, medieval romances, chivalric tales, social customs, beliefs, and legends. (Kumar, 2006)

Whether utilized in tandem with mass media or other media forms, or as a re-telling of a traditional fable, story or song with updated prosocial content, folk media can be used as an effective E-E/Edutainment media device, especially when applied towards a stakeholder demographic which may identify most readily with traditional cultural elements.

NEW MEDIA

The general term "New Media" includes emerging digital and ICTs (Information and Communication Technogies) geared towards delivery of Edutainment content; examples include internet-based and standalone video games and simulations, content delivered by mobile phones, and other non-traditional electronic media.

PC Magazine defines New Media as:

> (1) The forms of communicating in the digital world, which includes
> electronic publishing on CD-ROM, DVD, digital television and,
> most significantly, the Internet. It implies the use of desktop and
> portable computers as well as wireless, handheld devices. Most
> every company in the computer industry is involved with new media
> in some manner. Contrast with old media. See digital convergence.
>
> (2) The concept that new methods of communicating in the digital
> world allow smaller groups of people to congregate online and share,
> sell and swap goods and information. It also allows more people to
> have a voice in their community and in the world in general
> (Computer Language Co., Inc, 2009)

New Media can also be defined as:

> The emergence of digital, computerized, or networked information
> and communication technologies in the later part of the 20th century.
> Most technologies which are considered as "New Media" are digital,
> often having characteristics of being manipulatable, networkable,
> dense, compressible, and impartial. (Wikipedia, 2009)

E-E/Edutainment initiatives delivered over the Internet may be restricted in
developing countries due to a lack of IT infrastructure limitations, though this is
not always the case. Mobile telephone use, for instance, has rapidly increased in
rural areas of many developing countries, with mobile telephony infrastructure
even "leapfrogging" the implementation of traditional fixed-line technologies.

Digital divide issues persist in many developing countries regarding Internet
infrastructure, (and has even impacted the research and production of this report,
as cited in its 'Limitations' section). This digital divide continues to hamper the

feasibility of E-E/Edutainment interventions, including games and other content which depend upon the Internet for delivery via download and hosting on remote servers.

While many E-E/Edutainment games are hosted online, and therefore favor use in developed nations, standalone installers for E-E/Edutainment computer applications can still be delivered on a CD-Rom or DVD or other offline format. Computer applications can even come pre-installed in inexpensive, user-friendly laptops such as the XO-1, which the One Laptop Per Child initiative is promoting in Cambodia and other developing countries to increase computer literacy in the classroom and at home. (One Laptop Per Child, 2009)

In an early high-profile educational games initiative, the World Food Program in 2005 released a downloadable real-time strategy game called *Food Force*, which was billed as the "first humanitarian video game" (World Food Program, 2006) *Food Force* tasks the player is with the challenges of delivering vital food aid in an imaginary country called Sheylan:

> With tens of thousands of Sheylan's residents displaced and in urgent need of food aid, players are required to pilot helicopters on reconnaissance missions, airdrop high energy biscuits to internally displaced person (IDP) camps, negotiate with armed rebels on a food convoy run and use food aid to help rebuild villages. (World Food Program, 2006)

The original *Food Force* game is evidently geared towards a target audience that does not suffer from digital divide issues. The large file size (227 Megabytes) of *Food Force* is a prohibitive obstacle to any potential user in areas where Internet access is slow, unreliable, expensive – or absent. As a case in point, while downloading *Food Force* in order to research it for this report, I sat for several hours at a Phnom Penh Wi-Fi enabled café, over the course of several days. I installed software which enabled downloads to be resumed in the event a file could not be retrieved in one session (which I couldn't), or in the event a power outage interrupted internet service (which happened several times).

Functionality aspects aside, the E-E/Edutainment principles of *Food Force* are easy to discern. *Food Force*, with its well-produced interface and fairly advanced production values, strives to raise behavior-changing awareness in the player by encouraging them to participate in a reasonably engaging simulation of a food delivery effort.

One concern regarding the use of video games for E-E/Edutainment purposes would be the overall technical hurdles that must be overcome in order to connect a target stakeholder to the game. Ultimately, however, the game must be primarily *entertaining* in order to attract and retain the stakeholder while delivering its prosocial messages.

Highlighting this crucial dimension, another E-E/Edutainment game that I did manage to download and play fairly easily (due to its small file size) was *FatWorld.*

FatWorld is an E-E/Edutainment game (also referred to as a "game for change" by its programmers at Persuasive Games) which is designed to educate a player about proper nutrition and beneficial eating habits.

The player selects a character and chooses from a number of factors such as the character's age, any pre-existing health conditions, and demographic factors such as working class versus upper class origins. The character is then assigned tasks to conduct in the hypothetical town where the game takes place, tasks which are intended to raise awareness regarding nutrition and obesity issues.

FatWorld is deeply linked to a developed-world context, in that the player must choose between eating such foods as salmon wraps and pancakes, which are abundantly present in the well-stocked refrigerator of the character's home. In a developing country context, the primary concern of an individual (especially those living in the rural areas) might be whether there were *any* food or not to eat – not *what kind*, or at what risk its ingestion might eventually exact.

Although well conceived for its particular target users (who have the dubious privilege of dealing with obesity issues) *FatWorld* falls short in one key way: it is not especially *entertaining*, at least in the experience of this author. This is primarily due to the fact that the character's physical movement through the imaginary town of the *FatWorld* is frustratingly slow, at least too slow to engage this researcher.

This leads to another, important question which concerns the use of computer games for E-E/Edutainment purposes. Specifically: how do E-E/Edutainment games stack up against their "pure entertainment" counterparts which may be far more popular amongst the target stakeholder demographic?

Games which are commercially produced purely for entertainment purposes often are very well produced and engaging; yet commercially produced games also frequently feature violent and graphic antisocial content which may encroach on the desired target stakeholder demographic.

By way of example, the World Food Program's *Food Force* may find itself competing head-on with an extremely popular antisocial video game, such as Rockstar Games' *Grand Theft Auto*, for the attention of the target demographic. *Grand Theft Auto* is a commercially successful video game which graphically valorizes the theft of automobiles, random violence, and the pursuit of power as the game's character-avatar roams the largely antisocial – but extremely playable and therefore "entertaining"– environment of the game.

Rogers and Singhal (2002) refer to a phenomenon of **resistances**, which has some bearing in scenarios such as the hypothetical "*FoodForce* vs. *Grand Theft Auto*" scenario alluded to above. In brief, this term ("resistances") describes the various factors that may impede either the production or delivery of prosocial content, or the resulting volition by the target stakeholder to properly act upon the behavior-changing prosocial messages, even though they may in fact be received.

Resistances may occur in the **media production environment** (i.e., a TV production environment which is adverse to risking tried and true commercial formulas); they may occur in the **message environment** (for example, when a competing unaffiliated anti-social message blunts the impact of a simultaneously occurring prosocial message; and finally, resistances may occur in **reception** (a target stakeholder receives the prosocial message but either misinterprets it within his or her own pre-existing antisocial framework, or fails to act upon it).

By way of example, Rogers and Singhal (2002) refer to an instance in which an otherwise well-executed E-E/Edutainment campaign launched by John's Hopkins University's Population Communication Services was blunted, via resistance in the message environment, by a competing anti-social message from another, unaffiliated source. While JHU/PCS had produced and aired in Mexico a number one pop song promoting sexual abstinence (*Cuando Estemos Juntos*), the number two pop song at the same time, *No Control*, was a song which actually *celebrated* promiscuity.

In the hypothetical scenario involving *Food Force* and *Grand Theft Auto*, a resistance can similarly occur in the message environment when the impact of former's prosocial messages are dissipated, or distracted by, the antisocial messages promoted by *Grand Theft Auto*.

Antisocial media in all its forms can be engaging ("entertaining") because it intersects with the more contrary, destructive aspects of human nature (aka, "evil") which we all do arguably possess. Philosopher Friedrich Nietzsche (2009) asserts as much in many of his works, including his collection of essays and aphorisms, *Beyond Good and Evil*:

> It might even be possible that WHAT constitutes the value of those good and respected things, consists precisely in their being insidiously related, knotted, and crocheted to these evil and apparently opposed things – perhaps even in being essentially identical with them.

Nietzsche's position coincides with the abundance of antisocial (both real and fictional) characters inhabiting the mediasphere today, with the antisocial ("evil") characters often being equally, if not more, compelling as the prosocial ("good") characters.

In non-E-E/Edutainment media, (i.e., "pure entertainment"), antisocial behaviors are often given free reign in order to attract viewers and drive ratings. Whether *Faust*'s Mephistopheles, or the *Dark Knight*'s (Batman's) Joker, a strong antagonist or anti-hero is often essential for a compelling narrative. However, as

Barker and Sabido (2005) point out, this dichotomy also forms the basis for successful E-E/Edutainment interventions, especially those that depend on a serialized, melodramatic format such as TV or Radio dramas:

> Positive characters exhibit admirable, or pro-social behavior, perhaps promoting the education of girls, delaying marriage, or planning the spacing of their children. Negative characters are decidedly anti-social in their behavior – perhaps drinking to excess or philandering.

This dichotomy between positive and negative values – between 'good" and "evil", between social and antisocial - is then effectively parlayed into a prosocial effort by introducing "transitional", or ambivalent, characters with whom the (presumably ambivalent) audience of target stakeholders can identify:

> Then there are characters that are somewhere in between. They are the very important transitional characters who are most similar to the audience and with whom most of the audience will identify…

> …As their behavior shifts through the course of the drama, and as they adopt more pro-social behaviors, the audience is brought along with them, modeling itself after them. (Barker and Sabido, 2005)

Therefore, in E-E/Edutainment media, antisocial characters' behaviors must be carefully scripted to serve as constructive – rather than destructive – antipodes to the prosocial characterizations that exist to propagate the prosocial message of the media's producers.

MOBILE TELEPHONY

Another rapidly emerging area in New Media is mobile telephony. Mobile phones with increasingly media-rich capabilities are rapidly gaining users in rural areas of

58

many developing countries. (Bhavnani, Chiu, Subraminam, Janakiram, and Silarsky 2008)

> On the one hand, it is estimated that there are presently about 1.1 billion
> fixed broadband lines, with many people in developing countries not
> having fixed line access - but there are 4 billion mobile connections - and
> this number continues to grow. (UNESCO, 2009)

Mobile telephones can deliver E-E/Edutainment content, such interactive games related to health issues, while simultaneously delivering other useful, non-entertaining data such as weather reports, pesticide use updates, and crop prices.

In India, ZMQ Software Systems is producing E-E/Edutainment games for mobile phones which are designed to share prosocial messages about HIV and AIDS with a younger, targeted demographic. One such game, called *Safety Cricket: A Role-play based game on Cricket,* uses a cricket game as the basis for educating about HIV/AIDS. The developers describe the game elements, which link the components of a cricket game to HIV transmission factors:

> Balls will appear regularly on the air in three different rows in form of 4
> Safety symbols: Condom, Faithful Partner, HIV Information and AIDS
> Red Ribbon. You score runs for collecting these items. At the same time,
> Outs will appears in form of Unsafe Sex, Infected Blood Transfusion,
> HIV Virus, Infected Syringe and Company of bad friends. (Sun
> Developer Network, 2009)

The Woodrow Wilson International Center for Scholars in the United States sponsors a dedicated *Games for Health* project, which brings together researchers, game experts, and users to promote games as a way of improving health care. The project also collects best practices and conducts contests for developers of health care games. (Games for Health, 2009)

A UNESCO mobile phone initiative is currently underway, with the goal of analyzing the potential for mobile-friendly content to be generated by community media in the context of developing countries. The project seeks to allow mobile phone subscribers to participate in the shaping of E-E/Edutainment content via a built in user feedback mechanism.

UNESCO describes four overarching goals of their mobile telephony effort:

1. Best exploit the capabilities of mobile radio and TV as demonstrated in good practices from other initiatives, regions, etc;

2. Produce mobile-adapted content, e.g. educational games, breaking news, and development videos;

3. Produce voice-based wikis or repositories for the use of spoken content on mobiles (instead of video- or text-based content);

4. Develop systems to diffuse their content on mobile devices, for example by means of: direct downloads, streaming, RSS, video-on-demand, and live radio and video mobile broadcast. (ICT for Development, 2009)

As mentioned, the mobile telephony user base has rapidly expanded in recent years, with mobile infrastructure often bypassing intermediate landline infrastructure in developing countries. This is especially true in rural areas, where the installation of traditional landline systems is not deemed to be cost-effective.

An observational aside from the Cambodian context supports this: while producing a video documentary, *Crisis* (2005), for the NGO Forum on

Cambodia, I spent one of night at a Jarai (indigenous rural minority) family's house in a remote part of rural Ratanakiri province, Cambodia.

I observed little in the way of modern technology, except for the occasional Daelim brand moto which is ubiquitous throughout the country. The house had no toilet, not even a squat toilet – the nearby forest served this purpose.

The family owned no TV, and I could observe only a small portable radio. The male head of the family had, however, just purchased his first mobile phone; he and a neighbor spent hours throughout the evening learning its functions (and settling, finally, in the wee hours, on the most pleasing ringtone).

Finally, mobile telephony holds great promise as an emerging two-way medium, versus traditional one-way mass media broadcast models. Users themselves can help shape content that may be delivered, by providing instant feedback via voice, voice message, or by pressing a number or series of numbers on the phone's keypad.

MULTIMEDIA: A Hybrid of Several Forms

Many of the most comprehensive, and often most effective, E-E/Edutainment interventions utilize several media forms within a single strategic framework.

The UNICEF *Meena* initiative, for example, stands out as a significant example of a multimedia intervention with an animated cartoon series at its center. The

Meena Communication Initiative (MCI) uses a multi-media E-E/Edutainment approach to support the status, rights and treatment of girls in South Asia. The stories developed for the MCI revolve around the adventures of Meena, a nine year old South Asian girl, her brother Raju, her pet parrot Mithu, and members of her family and village community. (Chesterton, 2004)

Meena is presented in the series as a role model in actively promoting a change in relation to the rights of children, and particularly of girls. Messages conveyed cover issues such as education, health, gender equity and freedom from exploitation and abuse. By the end of 2003, twenty four stories had been produced; the key messages of some of the of these episodes are listed below:

1. *Count Your Chickens* Meena's dream of going to school comes true

5. *Saving a Life* Meena saves baby Rani when she has diarrhea

7. *Say No to Dowry* Meena and her family question the practice of dowry

9. *Take Care of Girls* Girls and boys have an equal right to health care

10. *I Love School* A good teacher makes all the difference

In Cambodia, eight *Meena* episodes have been dubbed into Khmer and shown on television, while in neighboring Viet Nam, *Meena* was translated into Vietnamese and the ethnic minority languages Bana, Khmer, H'mong and Tay (although the name 'Meena' was changed to the more locally relevant 'Mai'). (Chesterton, 2004) The program was shown in areas populated by ethnic minorities with poor access to information and services. Flipcharts, leaflets and cartoon books have also been adapted to fit the Vietnamese culture. Thus use of supporting materials, posters, etc compliments the E-E mass media content which is designed to spearhead the initiative.

Few health education projects have used a variety of mutually-supporting media forms so comprehensively as South Africa's *Soul City*, a primary health care initiative involving TV and radio soap operas with numerous multimedia support materials. *Soul City* was broadcast in a total of nine languages and was boosted by a vigorous public relations campaign involving talent competitions, newspaper articles, radio spots, and a multi media educational package aimed at health and educational workers. (Soul City Institute, 2009)

The live performance Ndere Troupe in Uganda has also utilized a multimedia approach with great effectiveness. The group has established a rural information network of five centers, hosted by farmer groups with direct communication access to its headquarters in Kampala. These information centers, called "InfoPops" relay requests to Ndere Troupe to develop plays on a particular social issue based on feedback from local communities.

Then, by way of a clever yet practical use of available resources:

> Ndere Troupe then develops the play and distributes the transcripts (generally, text and video) electronically to the InfoPops (on CD ROM through normal
> postal services). The InfoPops then channel the information via this theatrical performance to rural communities in local languages...
>
> ...The ICT facilities in the rural InfoPops are also used by the community for other purposes, for example to access market information, to give farmers information on new crops. (Tulp and de Jager, 2009)

(Note that activities along the lines of Ndere Troupe assume a functioning postal service and Internet access as key links in the distribution chain.)

The advantages of the live performance / Theater for Development approach utilized by Ndere Troupe and other organizations, is that the E-E/Edutainment content can be modified or adjusted in response to the localized needs of audience members. Live theater interventions can therefore respond quickly to particular, unanticipated inputs of data from target communities; conversely, large and complex mass media interventions must wait through a production cycle to incorporate changes in programming.

THEORETICAL ASPECTS OF E-E/EDUTAINMENT

Albert Bandura's Social Learning Theory is a key theory which underpins E-E/Edutainment interventions, and it is often cited as a primary influence by many practitioners and researchers alike. The theory explains how an individual in the socialization process learns by observing from others what behaviors are appropriate or viable, rather than learning only by "trial and error and suffering damage - or even death - as a result. Bandura (1969) elaborates:

> The provision of social models is also an indispensable means of trans-
> mitting and modifying behavior in situations where errors are likely to
> produce costly or fatal consequences. Indeed, if social learning
> proceeded exclusively on the basis of rewarding and punishing
> consequences, most people would never survive the socialization
> process.

This **identification process**, when elicited through E-E/Edutainment media through a variety of approaches and methodologies – including Miguel Sabido's highly effective and eponymous "Sabido Methodology" (Barker and Sabido,

2005) - allows a viewer, listener, reader, player, or other audience stakeholder to empathize with, and learn from, one or more of the characters who are strategically depicted in the media content in order to impart a prosocial lesson. As the character in an E-E/Edutainment intervention faces a series of challenges, difficulties, and experiences relevant to the key social issues being addressed, so too does the stakeholder undergo a vicarious learning experience, which may lead to the desired prosocial behavioral change. (Singhal and Svenkerud, 1994)

Besides TV and Radio dramas, other media forms can effectively elicit identification as well:

Theater, including E-E/Edutainment-oriented Theater for Development and Theater of the Oppressed (TO) type undertakings for example, is an ancient form of human expression, which has for thousands of years elicited identification ("Pathos") in spectator/audiences. Moreover, theater is the genealogical forbearer of other dramaturgic media forms including serialized TV, radio, and long-form feature films.

Traditional and folk media have been eliciting identification with hero-characters since the dawn of human expression, via spoken word fables, stories, and myths which have often served in an educational or instructive role.

More contemporarily, in the modern areas of **New Media,** the hero-avatar of a role-playing computer E-E/Edutainment game or simulation elicits identification in a player. As the character-avatar makes its way through a variety of challenges in the virtual environment of the game, the player (who may be also be actually physically guiding that character in real-time) can identify strongly with his or her onscreen reflection, in both an emotional and semi-physical sense as well.

So long as the onscreen character is learning to overcome challenges involving a social issue dimension in a significantly entertaining way the player may in turn identify with that character and learn those same prosocial lessons. (Taylor, 2003), (Cohen, 2001)

One unique strength of E-E/Edutainment is that it engages both the emotions *and* the rational thought processes; the emotions are particularly engaged when dramaturgical elements find their way into media interventions. For example, experiencing a favorite TV character die of AIDS, and watching his family subsequently grieve, may be more effective in changing an individual's behavior than any rational-didactic structured media message. (Rogers and Singhal, 2002), (Kort, Picard, and Reilly 2001)

Therefore, a part of E-E/Edutainment's power to change behavior lies in the emotional connection between the media character and the target stakeholder. This emotional connection leads in turn to the identification processes which Bandura describes (1969) thereby offering opportunities to insert prosocial behavior-change messages in the media, and ergo, target stakeholder.

Apwe Plezi, which aired in the Caribbean island-nation of St. Lucia from 1996 through the year 2000, refers to the Creole proverb "Apwe plezi c'est la pain," ("After the pleasure comes the pain"). This radio intervention was produced and broadcast to promote the use of family planning, the prevention of HIV and other sexually transmitted diseases (STDs), gender equity and other social development goals.

In their analysis of the intervention, Regis and Vaughan (2000) elaborate on the identification mechanism at work in the design of the programming:

> The characters in entertainment-education programs serve as positive, negative or transitional behavioral role models, and their fates provide vicarious learning experiences to demonstrate the consequences of alternative behaviors. Positive characters embody positive values and are rewarded…
>
> …In *Apwe Plezi*, for example, Leona is a well-educated woman of 23 who wants to delay childbearing until she is financially secure. Leona suspects that her boyfriend, Marcus, has other sexual partners, and she decides to break up with him because of her fear of contracting HIV from him. Leona eventually takes a job and marries Marcus, after he reforms. (Regis, St. Catherine, and Vaughan, 2000)

Similarly, negative character values are punished:

> The *Apwe Plezi* character Tony has multiple partners and children by two of them. He refuses to support his children, he rapes a woman on a date and ultimately he contracts HIV.

Alas, the fate of Tony – as devised by the writers, producers, donors, and other change agents behind the life of his character – is strategically designed to reinforce positive health behaviors in the listener by exploiting Bandura's identification process. In *Apwe Plezi*, by "witnessing" the death of Tony due to HIV/AIDS and vicariously feeling the subsequent grief of his family and friends, a listener may be motivated seek to avoid a similar fate by changing his or her own behavior.

Secondary, transitional characters, may be introduced as needed to further reinforce identification with "correct" or prosocial behavior:

> Transitional characters are torn between the positive and the negative values, but eventually choose the positive values and a rewarded. For example, Georgie is a young man who becomes a drug user and unintentionally impregnates his 16-yearold girlfriend, but who later

enters a drug rehabilitation program and tries to become more sexually responsible. (Regis, St. Catherine, and Vaughan, 2000)

One reason radio and TV serials (narratives) are persistently useful in many E-E/Edutainment roles is due to their inherent *mythologies*. Arvind Singhal points out that "The melodramatic serial embodies several characteristics of a mythical narrative. A mythical narrative is one that expressed, recreates, and gives voice to a myth." (Lozanzo and Singhal, 1993)

However, Western forms of myth and narrative may arguably collide with their non-Western counterparts, and vice-versa. This schism could in turn affect the ability of a TV serial to be transplanted or re-broadcast (through re-dubbing) from one geographic or cultural area to another.

While Bandura's social learning theory is applied frequently in serial narrative formats such as the radio or TV drama, any format that utilizes some form of characterization offers opportunities for identification between viewer/user/player and the character being portrayed. (Cohen, 2001) Indeed, the narrative is one of the defining aspects of humanity, and is a fundamental vehicle for communication, whether through spoken word or mass media formats. Walter Fischer's narrative theory, for instance, asserts that man "is essentially a storyteller" (Hinyard and Kreuter, 2007).

Narrative media forms are therefore ideal methods for communicating prosocial messages. These narrative functions are not confined to mass media only; as discussed earlier, an E-E/Edutainment novella, comic book, or video game offers opportunities for stakeholder identification, provided the main character and narrative is adequately developed and is genuinely engaging or interesting.

Additionally, effective E-E/Edutainment need not be confined to the narrative format, as the author's proposed Knowledge, Attitude, and Practice (KAP) survey [see section V.ii in this report] will seek to confirm.

TYPES OF DESIRED BEHAVIOR CHANGES

The goal of Entertainment-Education (E-E)/Edutainment is to effect a prosocial behavior change in target stakeholders. If prosocial behavior change is not adopted by the stakeholders to a significant degree, then an E-E/Edutainment intervention cannot be considered to be successful.

Rogers and Singhal (2002) propose various types of behavior change that may seek to be induced through exposure to E-E/Edutainment interventions:

a) **individual** versus **collective**

(b) **one-time** (e.g., getting an immunization) versus **recurring** (e.g., physical exercise)

(c) **self-controlled** (e.g., fastening an automobile seat belt) versus **other dependent** (e.g., paying and receiving dowry)

(d) **private** (e.g., using a condom) versus **public** (e.g., cleaning up an unsanitary neighborhood)

(e) **preventive** (e.g., using sunscreen) versus **curative** (e.g., administering oral rehydration therapy to a baby with diarrhea)

(f) **costly** (e.g., adopting a tractor) versus **low cost** (e.g., breast-feeding)

(g) **high involvement** (e.g., enrolling in an adult literacy class) versus **low involvement** (e.g., buying Girl Scout cookies) (Rogers and Singhal, 2002)

As the implementation of an E-E/Edutainment effort in the development context must result in an appreciable level of behavioral change in stakeholders, this degree of impact must be ultimately be measurable. Therefore, an impact assessment in some form is a key part of any overall E-E/Edutainment intervention, even while assessment techniques are still evolving.

WAYS TO ASSES EFFECTIVENESS OF E-E INTERVENTIONS

A common critique of using E-E/Edutainment approaches to promote prosocial behavior change is the difficulty in 1) predicting *which* audience members will change behaviors and 2) how to *quantify the amount* of behavior change which is actually created. Brown and Singhal (1996) cite the incorporation of more rigorous research designs as an important goal for future E-E/Edutainment practitioners and strategists.

Nonetheless, E-E/Edutainment practitioners can currently gauge the effectiveness of an intervention, whether a radio drama, television soap, theater for development, folk and traditional media, or New Media, through a variety of measures. Some of these approaches – such as the use of surveys - are standard to the development industry, while others adhere more closely to entertainment-oriented ratings systems.

While audience surveys have historically been used to assess the impact of E-E/Edutainment interventions, recent thinking suggest that surveys alone may not accurately reflect the degree and dimension of impact on target stakeholders. Rogers and Singhal (2002) refer to recent literature which supports the pursuit of a more *pluralistic* approach to measuring the results of interventions. The authors assert that focus groups, participant observation, interviews, and even ancillary materials such as unsolicited letters and call-ins from audience members should all be utilized as part of a holistic assessment effort.

In particular, unsolicited audience letters are especially useful in that they are unmediated and unbiased by researchers. (Rogers and Singhal, 2002) The author of this report is obliged to point out, however, that the assessment of audience letters assumes 1) a functioning postal service and 2) a literate viewing audience who 3) has the time, inclination, and postage money to write a letter and send it voluntarily.

The *degree of exposure* which an audience member experiences in any particular E-E/Edutainment intervention is also important to measure, as is the amount of interpersonal communication between audience members (directly exposed to content) and non-audience members (indirectly exposed through socialization), who may be receiving prosocial messages in a secondary way. For example, a particularly compelling and effective radio drama might provoke discussion between a listener, and his or her friends or family who had not tuned in to the program. (Rogers and Singhal, 2002)

The UNICEF *Meena* initiative uses several approaches in measuring the effects and impacts of its multimedia (cartoon, comic book, and supporting materials) intervention:

> In each country, a mix of quantitative and qualitative techniques was used to address the evaluation questions. Quantitative data were gathered from children and adults through household surveys, using structured interview schedules...Qualitative techniques consisted of document analysis, focus group discussions, interviews, workshops and meetings with people involved in or affected by the MCI. (UNICEF, 2009)

A post-campaign assessment of the prosocial radio soap opera, *Apwe Plezi*, which aired in the Caribbean island-nation of St. Lucia from 1996 through the year 2000, provides a thorough profile of the methodology used to assess the impact of that program's broadcasts.

> Our principal source of information about the program's effects was a pretest-posttest survey conducted through personal interviews…
>
> …Each survey included an independent quota sample that was representative of the country's sexually active population aged 15–54 (according to the 1991 census) in terms of geographic representation of the 10 districts of St. Lucia, sex ratio, age distribution and socioeconomic status. (Regis, St. Catherine, and Vaughan, 2000)

It may be interesting to note, in light of Rogers and Singhal's (2002) discussion of the importance of pluralistic assessment approaches, that neither listener letters nor phoned-in comments were apparently utilized in the stated assessment methodology for *Apwe Plezi*.

Chuyen Que Minh or "Homeland Story", was a rice pest management intervention launched in July 2004 in Vietnam, with the goal of educating rural farmers about the importance of proper pesticide applications in rice farming. The radio drama sought to enable farmers to better understand pest damages and make more informed, less wasteful, and ecologically damaging decisions involving pesticide use.

A post-program follow up survey was conducted to determine the impacts of the program:

> Prior to developing the questionnaire for each of these surveys, the authors conducted focus group discussions to gather materials to structure and frame the questionnaires. The questionnaires were prepared

in English, translated into Vietnamese and pre-tested before they were finalized. (Chien, Escalada, Heong, Huan, Ky Ba, Quynh, and Thiet, 2008)

The results of the survey indicated significant impact from the broadcasts:

> Our data showed that the entertainment-education soap opera, *Chuyen Que Minh,* contributed positively to changes in farmers' beliefs and practices…Farmers' belief that pesticides will affect their health increased from 62% to 86% indicating a positive change in attitudes towards good health. (Chien, Escalada, Heong, Huan, Ky Ba, Quynh, and Thiet, 2008)

Rogers and Singhal (2002) also discuss the use of special *markers* to gauge audience exposure to E-E/Edutainment content. Markers, which are distinct elements embedded within a prosocial message, may be created by introducing (for example) a particular product name in the media content or program. Along these lines, in *Apwe Plezi*, a fictitious new condom brand called "Catapult" was deliberately introduced into the storyline as a "marker":

> This new term ("Catapult") was identified by 28% of the radio program's listeners, validating their claim of direct exposure to the program, and by 13% of the non-listeners, suggesting that the message was diffused via interpersonal channels, and thus providing a test of diffusion of innovations theory. (Regis, St. Catherine, and Vaughan, 2000)

Markers in E-E/Edutainment media can also act in an auto-replicating fashion, in that they may become a self-perpetuating meme, sign, or phrase – which thereby boosts the indirect or secondary impacts of the intervention.

For example, one overly promiscuous character in a Jamaican AIDS awareness radio serial, *Naseberry Street,* was named "Scattershot". After repeated mention on the program, this name (Scattershot) worked its way into everyday local language, with the name being applied as a general descriptive term for someone who presented the same antisocial behaviors as the character from the radio drama. (Rogers and Singhal, 2002)

Finally, letter-writing or other forms of direct communication from the audience to the chief change agents involved in an E-E/Edutainment intervention are, as mentioned, recognized as a promising way to gauge audience or stakeholder responses.

> Letters written in response to an entertainment-education radio drama serial by listeners can help us understand how they know what they heard, and with what psychosocial consequences. (Law and Singhal, 1999)

The authors assessed the Indian radio drama, *Tinka Tinka Sukh* ('Happiness Lies in Small Things ') which was broadcast in India in 1996-7, and they describe their methodology in assessing letters that had been written in response to the program:

> An estimated 125,000-150,000 letters were received by AIR in response to *Tinka Tinka Sukh* during its one-year of broadcast. Clearly, audience members who wrote letters to *Tinka Tinka Sukh* represent a highly involved audience group, and are atypical of the total audience. We obtained a sample of approximately 5000 letters from AIR, from which we randomly selected 260 letters. These 260 letters were then quantitatively and qualitatively content analyzed (23 had to be discarded due to illegibility). (Law and Singhal, 1999)

A personal dimension of the impact of the program on audience stakeholders was revealed through an analysis of these voluntary, non-survey materials (the letters), supporting the pluralistic/holistic approach suggested by Rogers and Singhal (2002) previously. Anupam Ushni, a listener from Bhanulipur village in Hardoi district, wrote, describing one of the characters he had identified with in the radio program: 'Champa's family situation is exactly like mine. . . I had given up studies but after listening to Tinka Tinka Sukh, I started to study again.' (Law and Singhal, 1999)

Law and Singhal (1999) continue by summarizing the linkage between the individuals' own expressed changes in behavior, and the intended design of the program:

> Most of the 237 letters expressed how they had learned new information on family and social issues such as the importance of education and being a good citizen. Many wrote to say that the radio program had caused them to think and see personal issues differently. As the examples demonstrated earlier, changes in self-efficacy beliefs with regard to motivational, affective and behavioral aspects also emerged.

The authors conclude that one of the greatest values of unsolicited feedback from an E-E/Edutainment intervention can be the unbiased nature of the writer's contribution. Letters and direct feedback significantly supplement a survey-only approach to any intervention's assessment.

> …in the absence of any reliable apparatus to assess the communicative dimensions of efficacy, these reports of the letter-writers are still significant for many reasons. They are informally written and the writers are not aware of a grand research design or motive. (Law and Singhal, 1999)

Even when audience letter-writing is minimal, a survey assessment can confirm correlations between prosocial content, audience/stakeholder exposure, and behavior change. This can be applied to non-mass media interventions as well, such as street theater:

> …The performances also changed attitudes of audience members toward people with AIDS. Before the performances 29% said they would shun

people with AIDS, 8% said they would turn them over to the police, and 18% said they would treat them the same as other people. After the performances 10% said they would shun, none said they would involve the police, and 50% said they would treat people with AIDS the same as others. (Johns Hopkins Bloomberg School of Public Health, 2008)

Caller feedback, via a specially established telephone hotline, is also an important tool in gauging the effectiveness of mass media campaigns. Many E-E/Edutainment interventions incorporate such call-in lines in the design of the overall strategy for this purpose. A call-in mechanism may also be used to modify future content in order to more effectively address the audience stakeholders' needs. Call-in numbers may also provide unexpected, related insights into other related aspects of an audience member's life, which may have qualitative bearing on either future productions or other aspects of the intervention.

The post-broadcast assessments of the radio serial *Apwe Plezi*: offers insight into this dimension:

> About 10 people called the *Apwe Plezi* hotline each week. Some offered advice to the characters (e.g., suggesting that one character put her child up for adoption); others gave compelling testimony about how they had suffered similar fates to those of the characters, including beatings and rape by their partner. (Regis, St. Catherine, and Vaughan, 2000)

This discussion of general impact assessment approaches leads to the final component of this paper: a proposed Knowledge, Attitude, and Practices (KAP) survey designed to determine the effects of a prosocial E-E/Edutainment which is specifically tailored to the Cambodian context.

VI.ii.2 *(Further Research):* KNOWLEDGE, ATTITUDE, and PRACTICE (KAP) SURVEY

The author recommends, as suggested in the ***Limitations*** section of this report, that further research (and practice) in E-E/Edutainment areas in Cambodia could best be done by native Khmer speakers or foreigner researchers with native-level fluency. A workable point of departure for such explorations might be achieved through an accessible and easily managed but effective methodology: the KAP (Knowledge, Attitude, and Practice) Survey

KAP survey is a long-standing methodology for measuring and analyzing the **diffusion of innovations**, with which Everett Rogers (1983) is closely associated.

The diffusion of innovations may be described as "the process by which an innovation is communicated through certain channels over time among the members of a social system." (Rogers, 1983). Since an innovation may rightfully include *any* concept or idea which is perceived as being new to a particular community or social system, it follows that a new prosocial concept -such as the use of condoms, or a particular high-yield agricultural technique - may be considered to be an innovation.

When an innovation is introduced to a social system, it is adopted by different members of the system at varying rates. Some members of the social system ("innovators") will adopt the innovation very rapidly, whereas others ("laggards') will adopt the innovation very slowly – or not at all, assuming that adoption of the innovation is voluntary.

The diffusion of these prosocial innovations can be tracked and studied using a variety of methodologies, including the KAP survey. The advantage of this research approach is its comparative simplicity of method, and the value which it provides in data on the dissemination and adoption process.

Traditionally, KAP surveys have been used particularly in studying agricultural extension and the adoption of "recommendation packages" of seeds, cultivation and pest and weed control systems in cash crops, and in the dissemination and adoption of health practices – e.g. in mother child health and in STD awareness and prevention.

PROJECT

The proposed KAP survey, proposed by the sponsor of this paper, Camerado SE Asia, is predicated on the execution of an E-E/Edutainment intervention utilizing prosocial messages delivered on the back of standard playing cards. The target stakeholder demographic will be motodop (freelance, unregistered motorcycle taxi) drivers who operate in a range of urban and peri-urban areas of Cambodia.

The project will be undertaken under the control of an independent civil society group working in the fields of health care and HIV/AIDS and STD awareness and prevention in Cambodia. The assessment survey will be undertaken at intervals of three and six months after the launch of the project.

The survey will be administered through face-to-face interviews using a structured questionnaire with a random sample of 20% of motodop drivers in one central area of Phnom Penh, and three other provincial urban areas in Cambodia that will have been exposed to the intervention. The number of interviewees would depend on a test of statistical significance, and is expected to be not less than 400 individuals.

The questionnaire will have four sections:

1. Knowledge of recommended practice in the use of condoms with sexual partners, and source of knowledge;

2. Attitude to the benefits of adoption and of risks related to failure to follow recommended practice;

3. Past practice in sexual relationships;

4. Present and intended future practice.

The analysis of the survey data will be analyzed using the SPSS platform.

CONCEPT

The concept underlying this project will be to explore the feasibility of local, real-world environments and their associated media potentialities (i.e., motodops playing cards on the streets of Cambodia in urban and peri-urban areas) in order to develop, as a methodological approach, the use of targeted (or "niche") non-mass media E-E/Edutainment interventions in a variety of scenarios.

DISSEMINATION

The main proposed dissemination of the data will be (a) provision to the sponsoring Cambodian civil society group, (b) provision to Ministry of Health/CHADS program, and (c) distribution by internet and in hard copy to academic bodies in Cambodia and abroad.

REFERENCES

AsiaPulse News (2000) 'VCD PLAYER MARKET BOOMING IN CHINA'S RURAL AREAS', retrieved from http://www.highbeam.com/doc/1G1-62500121.html (Accessed October 2009)

Bandura, A. (1969) 'Social-Learning Theory Of Identificatory Processes' in Goslin, David A. (ed.) *Handbook of Socialization Theory and Research:* Rand McNally & Company

Barker, K. and Sabido, Miguel (2005) 'Soap Operas for Social Change to Prevent HIV/AIDS: A Training Guide for Journalists and Media Personnel' on *The Communications Initiative Website* retrieved from *http://www.comminit.com/en/node/283890/304* Population Media Center, Shelburne, VT

Benjamin, W. (2002) 'Art In a Technological Age' (*Das Kunstwerk im Zeitalter Seiner Technischen Reproduzierbarkeit*), in Eiland, H and Jennigs, M (eds) 'Selected Writings', Volume 3, 1935-1938 Belknap Press of Harvard University Press, Massachusetts. Originally published in *Zeitschrift für Sozialforschung, 1936*

Bhasin, U., Saumya, P., and Singhal, A. (2002) 'USING RADIO DRAMA TO ENTERTAIN AND EDUCATE: INDIA'S EXPERIENCE WITH THE PRODUCTION, RECEPTION, AND TRANSCREATION OF "DEHLEEZ", in Journal of Development Communication 13(2), pp. 52-66

Bhavnani, A., Rowena, Won-Wai Chiu, Subraminam, Janakiram, and Silarsky, P. (2008) 'The Role of Mobile Phones in Sustainable Rural Poverty Reduction' in *World Bank Report, June 2008.* World Bank, GICT Department

Boal, A. (1993) *Theater of the Oppressed.* Theater Communications Group, New York, NY.

Brown, W.J., and Singhal, A. (1990) 'Ethical Dilemmas of Prosocial Television' in *Communication Quart*erly, 38(3) pp 268-230

Chesterton, P. (2004) *Evaluation of the Meena Communication Initiative.* UNICEF Regional Office for South Asia

Chien, H.V., Escalada, M.M., Heong, K.L., Huan, N.H., Ky Ba, V. H., Quynh, P.V., and Thiet (2008) 'Entertainment-Education and rice pest management: A radio soap opera in Vietnam' in *Crop Protection 27 pp. 1392-1397*

Cohen, J. (2001) 'Defining Identification: A Theoretical Look at the Identification of Audiences with Media Characters' in *Mass Media & Society* 4(3) 245-264. University of Haifa

Computer Language Company Inc. (2009) 'Definition of New Media' in PCMag.com. Retrieved from http://www.pcmag.com/encyclopedia_term/0,2542,t=new+media&i=47936,00.asp Ziff Davis (accessed October 2009)

Crystalinks.com (2009) 'Ancient Greek Theater' retrieved from http://www.crystalinks.com/greektheater.html (accessed October 2009)

Daudu, S. (2009) 'Problems and Prospect of Folk Media Usage for Agricultural Extension Service Delivery in Benue State, Nigeria' in *J Hum Ecol*, 25(1): 19-24 Kamla-Raj

DVD Burning Biz (2004) 'DVD and VCD Data Specifications' retrieved from http://www.dvdburning.biz (accessed October 2009)

Games For Health (2009), retrieved from http://www.gamesforhealth.org/about2.html (accessed October 2009)

Hinyard, L., Kreuter, M. (2007) 'Narrative Communication as a Tool for Health Behavior Change: A Conceptual, Theoretical, and Empirical Overview' in *Health Education & Behavior* 34(5) pp. 777-792 Health Communication Research Laboratory and Center for Cultural Cancer Communication, School of Public Health, Saint Louis University, Missouri

ICT for Development (2009) 'Applied Research on the Use and Potential for Mobile-friendly Content of Community Media' from Lourenco, Mirta (summary of email May 22, 2009) and *UNESCO to Help Community Media with Mobile Content Production* (2009). ICT website, accessed October 2009

Johns Hopkins Bloomberg School of Public Health Programs (2008). *From Drama to Games: A Range of E-E Formats.* February 2008, Issue 17

Johns Hopkins Bloomberg School of Public Health's INFO Project Center for Communication Programs (2008), 'Entertainment Education for Better Health' Retrieved from *Info For Health website* http://www.infoforhealth.org/inforeports/E-E/3.shtml (17), Baltimore

Kort, B., Picard, R., and Reilly, R. (2001) 'An Affective Model of Interplay Between Emotions and Learning: Reengineering Educational Pedagogy—Building a Learning Companion' in *Advanced Learning Technologies, Proceedings IEEE International Conference on Publication.* MIT Media Lab, Cambridge, MA.

Kumar, H. (2006) 'Folk Media and Rural Development' in *Indian Media Studies Journal* 1(1) July-Dec. 2006. Maharishi Dayanand University

Law, S and Singhal, A. (1999) 'EFFICACY IN LETIER- WRITING TO AN ENTERTAINMENT-EDUCATION RADIO SERIAL' in *Gazette* 61(5), Sage Publications, London

Learning Theories Knowledgebase (2009) *Social Learning Theory (Bandura)* Retrieved December 18th 2009 from http://www.learning-theories.com/social-learning-theory-bandura.html

LICADHO (Cambodian League for the Promotion and Defence of Human Rights) (2008) *Reading Between the Lines: How Politicas, Money & Fear Control Cambodia's Media.* Licadho, Cambodia

Lozanzo, E. and Singhal, S. (1993) 'Melodramatic Serials: Mythical Narratives for Education' in *Communications: The European Journal of Communication* 18(1)

Mahesh, P. (2007) *Social Marketing: A Communication Tool For Development,* proceedings of International Marketing Conference on Marketing & Society, 8-10 April, 2007, IIMK

Marshfield, K and van Oosterhout, M. (2007) 'Survey of Content and Audiences of Video Halls in Uganda' summarized in *African Movies Forum* by Musinguzi, B (ed) retrieved from http://www.nollywood.net/vbee/showthread.php?t=1050 Making African Movies forum], [http://www.africafiles.org/article.asp?ID=19215 (accessed October 2009)

Mok, K.D. (2009) 'Karaoke: From Cheesy Entertainment to Environmental Education Tool' Treehugger.com, retrieved from http://www.treehugger.com/files/2009/02/karaoke-effective-environmental-education-tool-cambodia.php (accessed October 2009)

Murphy, S. and Cody, M. (eds.) (2003) *Developing a Research Agenda for Entertainment Education and Multicultural Audiences,* Proceedings of A conference sponsored by The Centers for Disease Control and Prevention Hollywood, Health & Society USC Annenberg Norman Lear Center, May 21-22, 2003 Santa Monica, California

Museum of Broadcast Communications, 'Definition of Development Communications'. Accessed at the Museum of Broadcast Communications Website at http://www.museum.tv/archives/etv/D/htmlD/developmentc/developmentc.htm (accessed October, 2009)

Ngenge, T. (2003) *SEX, AIDS and VIDEOTAPE VIDEO AS A TOOL IN INFORMING ABOUT HIV/AIDS AMONG YOUNG PEOPLE IN RURAL MOZAMBIQUE.* Malmo University

NGO Forum on Cambodia (exec. producers). 'CRISIS: Land Alienation in Ratanakiri Province', 2005. Produced by Camerado, viewable at: http://video.google.com/videoplay?docid=-8513410690808029611&ei=_rk6S6vXPJSWwgPOo9TaCA&q=crisis+ratanakiri

Niedermier, J., Novotny, Olivia P., Papadopoulos, N., Pawuk, M., Pope, N., Ralston, R., Sipe, M. (2004) 'Censorship of TV and Radio' in *Group 6 Project Report,* retrieved from http://www.bgsu.edu/departments/tcom/faculty/ha/tcom103fall2004/gp6/gp6.pdf. Bowling Green State University.

Nietzsche, F. (2009) 'Beyond Good and Evil' from Zimmern, H. (translator), *The Complete Works of Friedrich Nietzsche* (Original publish date 1886) Retrieved from http://www.gutenberg.org/4/3/6/4363/ Project Gutenberg Edition, 2009

One Laptop Per Child (2009) 'Software', retrieved from OLPC Website http://laptop.org/en/laptop/software/index.shtml (accessed October 2009)

RDI Cambodia (accessed 2009). 'Why Karaoke Works'. Retrieved from http://www.rdic.org/studiopage.htm RDI Cambodia

Regis, A., St. Catherine, E., and Vaughan, P. W. (2000) 'Effects of an Entertainment-Education Radio Soap Opera on Family Planning And HIV Prevention in St. Lucia' in *International Family Planning Perspectives* 26(4): pp148-157

Rogers, E. M. (1983). *Diffusion of Innovations* (3rd edition). New York: Free Press.

Rogers, E. and Singhal, A. (2002) 'A Theoretical Agenda for Entertainment-Education' in *Communication Theory* 12(2): pp 117-135

Singhal, A. (2002) 'Harnessing the Entertainment-Education Strategy in Africa: The Soul City Intervention in South Africa' in Okigbo, Charles (ed.) *Development and Communication in Africa,* Rowman and Littlefield

Singhal, A. and Svenkerud, P. J. (1994) 'PRO-SOCIALLY SHAREABLE ENTERTAINMENT TELEVISION PROGRAMMES: A Programming Alternative in Developing Countries?', *The Journal of Development Communication* 2(5) pp. 17-30

Soul City Institute (2009) 'Soul City Programmes' Retrieved from the Soul City Institute website http://www.soulcity.org.za/programmes/the-soul-city-series/ (Accessed November, 2009)

Stearns, C. Z., and Stearns, P. N. (1988). Emotion and Social Change: Toward a New Psychohistory [Book, Holmes & Meier] In *Media-Culture.org*. Retrieved from http://wiki.media-culture.org.au/index.php/E-Learning_-_Edutainment

Sun Developer Network (2009) *ZMQ Launches Four Mobile Games on HIV/AIDS Awareness.* Retrieved from http://developers.sun.com/asiasouth/features/zmq_hivawareness.html (accessed October 2009)

Taylor, L. (2003) 'When Seams Fall Apart: Video Game Space and the Player' in *International Journal of Computer Game Research* 3(2)

The Communications Initiative Network (2006) Retrieved from http://www.comminit.com/en/node/303572 (accessed October 2009)

Tufte, T. (2003) *Telenovelas, Culture and Social Change-from Polisemy, Pleasure and Resistance to Strategic Communication and Social Development* [Publisher N/A pursuant to inquiry with author]

Tulp, E. and de Jager, A. (pub. date N/A) *Using Dance, Drama and ICTs to Inform Rural Communities: The ARRIN Project* (accessed 2009)

TV and Film Violence Reaches a New High in 2006' (2007) Updated December, 2007' accessed at the Cyber College website http://www.cybercollege.com/violence.htm (October, 2009)

UNICEF (accessed 2009) 'Meena Communication Initiative'. Retrieved from http://www.unicef.org/rosa/media_2479.htm (accessed 2009)

UNESCO (2009) 'UNESCO to Help Community Media with Mobile Content Production', in *Applied Research on the Use and Potential for Mobile-friendly Content of Community Media.* Retrieved from the Communications Initiative Network website at http://www.comminit.com/en/node/294122/38 (accessed November 2009)

VideoHelp.com (1999-2007) 'Video Formats Comparison' retrieved from http://www.videohelp.com/oldguides/comparison (accessed October 2009)

Visit CAMERADO online at
http://www.camerado.com
for more information on
innovative Edutainment media

Made in the USA
Coppell, TX
09 August 2024

35773320R00050